THE GREEK TRAGEDY
IN NEW TRANSLATIONS

GENERAL EDITORS
Peter Burian and Alan Shapiro

EURIPIDES: Cyclops

EURIPIDES

Cyclops

Translated by
HEATHER McHUGH
With Introduction and Notes by
DAVID KONSTAN

OXFORD
UNIVERSITY PRESS

2001

OXFORD
UNIVERSITY PRESS

Oxford   New York
Athens   Auckland   Bangkok   Bogotá   Buenos Aires   Calcutta
Cape Town   Chennai   Dar es Salaam   Delhi   Florence   Hong Kong   Istanbul
Karachi   Kuala Lumpur   Madrid   Melbourne   Mexico City   Mumbai
Nairobi   Paris   São Paulo   Shanghai   Singapore   Taipei   Tokyo   Toronto   Warsaw

and associated companies in
Berlin   Ibadan

Published by Oxford University Press, Inc.
198 Madison Avenue, New York, New York 10016

Oxford is a registered trademark of Oxford University Press

Library of Congress Cataloging-in-Publication Data
Euripides.
[Cyclops. English]
Euripides : Cyclops / translated by Heather McHugh, with introduction and notes by
David Konstan.
p.   cm.
ISBN 0-19-514303-5 (pbk.)
1. Cyclopes (Greek mythology)—Drama.   2. Greek drama (Satyr play)   I. McHugh,
Heather, 1948–   II. Konstan, David.   III. Title.
PA3975.C9 M39   2001
882'.01—dc21

00-055767

9 8 7 6 5 4 3 2 1
Printed in the United States of America

EDITORS' FOREWORD

"The Greek Tragedy in New Translations is based on the conviction that poets like Aeschylus, Sophocles, and Euripides can only be properly rendered by translators who are themselves poets. Scholars may, it is true, produce useful and perceptive versions. But our most urgent present need is for a *re-creation* of these plays—as though they had been written, freshly and greatly, by masters fully at home in the English of our own times."

With these words, the late William Arrowsmith announced the purpose of this series, and we intend to honor that purpose. As was true of most of the volumes that began to appear in the 1970s—first under Arrowsmith's editorship, later in association with Herbert Golder—those for which we bear editorial responsibility are products of close collaboration between poets and scholars. We believe (as Arrowsmith did) that the skills of both are required for the difficult and delicate task of transplanting these magnificent specimens of another culture into the soil of our own place and time, to do justice both to their deep differences from our patterns of thought and expression and to their palpable closeness to our most intimate concerns. Above all, we are eager to offer contemporary readers dramatic poems that convey as vividly and directly as possible the splendor of language, the complexity of image and idea, and the intensity of emotion of the originals. This entails, among much else, the recognition that the tragedies were meant for performance—as scripts for actors—to be sung and danced as well as spoken. It demands writing of inventiveness, clarity, musicality, and dramatic power. By such standards we ask that these translations be judged.

This series is also distinguished by its recognition of the need of nonspecialist readers for a critical introduction informed by the best recent scholarship, but written clearly and without condescension.

Each play is followed by notes designed not only to elucidate obscure references but also to mediate the conventions of the Athenian stage as well as those features of the Greek text that might otherwise go unnoticed. The notes are supplemented by a glossary of mythical and geographical terms that should make it possible to read the play without turning elsewhere for basic information. Stage directions are sufficiently ample to aid readers in imagining the action as they read. Our fondest hope, of course, is that these versions will be staged not only in the minds of their readers but also in the theaters to which, after so many centuries, they still belong.

A NOTE ON THE SERIES FORMAT

A series such as this requires a consistent format. Different translators, with individual voices and approaches to the material in hand, cannot be expected to develop a single coherent style for each of the three tragedians, much less make clear to modern readers that, despite the differences among the tragedians themselves, the plays share many conventions and a generic, or period, style. But they can at least share a common format and provide similar forms of guidance to the reader.

1. Spelling of Greek names

Orthography is one area of difference among the translations that requires a brief explanation. Historically, it has been common practice to use Latinized forms of Greek names when bringing them into English. Thus, for example, Oedipus (not Oidipous) and Clytemnestra (not Klutaimestra) are customary in English. Recently, however, many translators have moved toward more precise transliteration, which has the advantage of presenting the names as both Greek and new, instead of Roman and neoclassical importations into English. In the case of so familiar a name as Oedipus, however, transliteration risks the appearance of pedantry or affectation. And in any case, perfect consistency cannot be expected in such matters. Readers will feel the same discomfort with "Athenai" as the chief city of Greece as they would with "Platon" as the author of the *Republic*.

The earlier volumes in this series adopted as a rule a "mixed" orthography in accordance with the considerations outlined above. The most familiar names retain their Latinate forms, the rest are transliterated; *–os* rather than Latin *–us* is adopted for the termination of masculine names, and Greek diphthongs (such as Iphige*nei*a for Latin Iphigenia) are retained. Some of the later volumes continue this practice, but where translators have preferred to use a more consistent practice of transliteration or Latinization, we have honored their wishes.

2. Stage directions

The ancient manuscripts of the Greek plays do not supply stage directions (though the ancient commentators often provide information relevant to staging, delivery, "blocking," etc.). Hence stage directions must be inferred from words and situations and our knowledge of Greek theatrical conventions. At best this is a ticklish and uncertain procedure. But it is surely preferable that good stage directions should be provided by the translator than that readers should be left to their own devices in visualizing action, gesture, and spectacle. Ancient tragedy was austere and "distanced" by means of masks, which means that the reader must not expect the detailed intimacy ("He shrugs and turns wearily away," "She speaks with deliberate slowness, as though to emphasize the point," etc.) that characterizes stage directions in modern naturalistic drama.

3. Numbering of lines

For the convenience of the reader who may wish to check the English against the Greek text or vice versa, the lines have been numbered according to both the Greek text and the translation. The lines of the English translation have been numbered in multiples of ten, and these numbers have been set in the right-hand margin. The notes that follow the text have been keyed to the line numbers of the translation. The (inclusive) Greek numeration will be found bracketed at the top of the page. Readers will doubtless note that in many plays the English lines outnumber the Greek, but they should not therefore conclude that the translator has been unduly prolix. In most cases the reason is simply that the translator has adopted the free-flowing norms of modern Anglo-American prosody, with its brief-breath- and emphasis-determined lines, and its habit of indicating cadence and caesuras by line length and setting rather than by conventional punctuation. Other translators have preferred to cast dialogue in more regular five-beat or six-beat lines, and in these cases Greek and English numerations will tend to converge.

Durham, N.C   PETER BURIAN
Chapel Hill, N.C.   ALAN SHAPIRO
2000

CONTENTS

CYCLOPS

INTRODUCTION

I. SATYR PLAY

When tragedy was performed in classical Athens (we are speaking here of the fifth century B.C.), each of three competing playwrights staged, on successive days, a set of four plays, called a tetralogy, at the major dramatic festival of the year. The first three were proper tragedies: they might make up a continuous story, as in Aeschylus' *Oresteia,* or else be unrelated in plot, like the *Bacchae,* the *Iphigenia in Aulis,* and the (lost) *Alcmaeon* of Euripides, mounted together in a single (posthumous) performance. The fourth play in the series, however, was something different: This was the satyr play, a burlesque version of a traditional myth, named for the chorus of satyrs or half-human figures — they are goats or horses from the waist down — that was specific to the genre (it is possible that some satyr plays lacked satyrs, but if so, these exceptions were few). One supposes that by this device the grim mood of tragedy was lifted before the audience went home for lunch. One ancient critic (Demetrius, in his essay "On Style," 169) neatly characterized satyr drama as "tragedy at play." But perhaps the element of parody in the satyr play had a deeper significance, offering not so much farce or escapism as a kind of joyful triumph, in which man rescues god instead of abjectly enduring what the gods send.[1]

The only satyr play to survive entire is Euripides' *Cyclops.* There are substantial fragments of some others: Sophocles' *Trackers,* for example (the recent adaptation of this play by Tony Harrison, under the title *The Trackers of Oxyrhynchus,* was a remarkable success), and Aeschylus' *Net-Fishers,* both recovered from papyrus dumps, but Euripides' is the only one to be transmitted by way of continuously copied manuscripts.

---

1. On the satyr play in general, see Dana F. Sutton, *The Greek Satyr Play* (Meisenheim: Hain, 1980).

Why it was selected for transcription by Byzantine scholars and teachers is unknown.

To judge from the *Cyclops*, satyr plays were short: At just over seven hundred verses, this one is about half the length of a typical Greek tragedy, and barely counts as a one-act play on the modern stage. It appears that the scene was usually set in some remote place—an island or a deserted seashore—where one might expect to encounter these Panlike creatures; in the *Cyclops*, the action is located on the island of Sicily, near Mount Aetna, the great volcano that erupted violently early in the fifth century B.C. It is not the real Sicily of Euripides' own time, however, but a mythical place, populated by the giant Cyclopes, (three syllables) who were imagined, in some accounts, as forging Zeus' thunderbolts in the furnace of the volcano. This faraway, semiprimitive location is quite different from the setting of Greek tragedy, which was characteristically in front of a royal palace or other populated site, though there are exceptions to this rule: Think of the isolated crag to which Prometheus is tied in the play *Prometheus Bound* (attributed to Aeschylus, but likely to be a posthumous adaptation by Aeschylus' son of one of his father's unfinished works).

Satyrs painted on vases are often shown wearing short, furry pants with an arc of a horsetail at their rears and, sometimes, an erect penis sticking out in front. They were supposed to be sons of Silenus, who, like them, had equine or caprine accoutrements.[2] Silenus was the boon and boozy companion of Dionysus (Bacchus), the god associated with wine, revelry, masks, and mystery; sometimes, he was represented as Dionysus' foster-parent. The satyrs' connection with the festive wine-god contributed to the air of lasciviousness and celebration that attaches to them in the satyr dramas. The trajectory of the satyr plays in general seems to have been from captivity to liberation, as they overcome their separation from the source of joyous frivolity and are reunited with their convivial deity. At all events, this is the pattern of the *Cyclops*. Dionysus was also the patron god of the theater—his priests sat front and center at each dramatic performance—and the theatrical entertainment was part of a festival in his honor. It would appear that the plots of the satyr plays, more than those of either tragedy or comedy, best corresponded to the ritual occasion.

---

2. For representations of satyrs in art, see François Lissarrague, "Why Satyrs Are Good to Represent," in John J. Winkler and Froma Zeitlin, eds., *Nothing to Do with Dionysus?* (Princeton: Princeton University Press, 1990) 228–36.

II. PRODUCTION

The Athenian theater was part of a holiday ceremony, sponsored by the state, and it differed in important ways from modern dramatic productions. To begin with, a playwright presented his work, perhaps in summary form, to a state official, whose responsibility it was to select the submissions of three dramatists for performance at one of the two citywide festivals: the Great Dionysia, held in early spring, which was the only one to feature satyr plays, and the Lenaea, which took place at the onset of winter (December-January), and again related to Dionysus, as indicated by his cult title, Lenaeus. In the case of comedies, the archon, as the official was called, chose one play from each playwright; the tragedians, as we have seen, submitted sets of four for the Great Dionysia, concluding with the satyr play (playwrights wrote either comedies or tragedies, not both). Once the selection was made, the official assigned to each playwright a troupe of actors—early on, just two, but in Euripides' time a company of three—and a chorus, made up of Athenian citizens. The expenses of training and outfitting the chorus for the citywide performances were undertaken by individual rich citizens and were treated as a kind of tax, like the responsibility of providing the rigging for a naval ship. A trainer was assigned to each chorus, and rehearsals could be time consuming and intense.

The actual performances at the Great Dionysia were preceded and followed by ritual events in honor of Dionysus. On the day before the shows, there was a procession to and from a nearby village called Eleutherae (related to the Greek word for freedom). There was also a public preview of the subjects of the plays, in which the dramatists and actors took a bow. Finally, there was a grand parade in town culminating in a sacrifice of bulls. In Euripides' time, if not earlier, there were also ceremonies in the theater before the performances proper. These included a libation by the ten elected Athenian generals, an announcement of public awards for especially deserving citizens, and a display of the tribute that had been paid by the subject states in Athens' empire; in addition, war orphans who had reached military age, and who had been raised at state expense, were presented in full armor. Theater was a political event as much as a religious expession and a form of entertainment.[3]

At a typical festival, the performances began early in the morning

---

3. For the festival context of the dramatic performances, see Simon Goldhill, "The Great Dionysia and Civic Ideology," in John J. Winkler and Froma Zeitlin, eds., *Nothing to Do with Dionysus?* (Princeton: Princeton University Press, 1990) 97–129.

and were over by midday. Tragic competitors had a day to themselves, for the exhibition of their four plays (three tragedies plus a satyr play); the comic playwrights, who mounted only one comedy each, all competed on a single day. In addition to the dramatic performances, however, there were contests involving a kind of choral song called a dithyramb. The Athenians were divided into ten broad associations, called tribes, and each tribe mounted both a men's and a boys' chorus. Since these choruses were made up of fifty people each, a quick calculation indicates that one thousand Athenians participated in the dithyrambic competitions alone. To these we must add the choruses in the tragedies and comedies (if we assume that they numbered fifteen each, we get ninety more) and the actors, not to mention a supporting cast of silent supernumeraries, flute players and other musicians, scenery artists, stagehands, judges to choose a winner among the competitors, and who knows how many others. It begins to look as though a good percentage of the Athenian male population was involved simply in putting on the show.[4]

The theater of Dionysus, where the festival of the Great Dionysia was celebrated, was at the foot of the acropolis and probably held as many as twenty-five thousand people. This number represents, on a reasonable estimate, something approaching the total adult male citizen body of Athens. It is unknown whether women attended the theater in Euripides' time (what evidence there is points both ways). But whether they did or did not, the Athenian theater was a huge spectacle, comparable not so much to modern Broadway as to the Super Bowl in the United States or the World Cup in soccer everywhere else. Practically everyone was there to watch.[5]

Physically, the theater was in the shape of a semicircle, slightly prolonged in front and tapering inward. The backdrop, behind the acting area (which was probably on a low, elongated platform in Euripides' time), cut the circle like a chord at the stage end. The seats rose up in tiers, separated by aisles that divided the audience space into wedges. We do not know in what order the general public was seated; it may have been randomly, first come first served (there was a small fee for attendance). I have already mentioned that the priests of Dionysus sat

4. General information on the dramatic festivals may be found in A. W. Pickard-Cambridge, *The Dramatic Festivals of Athens*, 2nd edition, revised by J. Gould and D. M. Lewis (Oxford: Oxford University Press, 1988); for translations of the texts cited in Pickard-Cambridge and further commentary, see also Eric Csapo and William J. Slater, *The Context of Ancient Greek Drama* (Ann Arbor: University of Michigan Press, 1995).

5. See further Simon Goldhill, "The Audience of Athenian Tragedy," in P. E. Easterling, ed., *The Cambridge Companion to Greek Tragedy* (Cambridge: Cambridge University Press, 1997) 54–68.

in the front row along with other civic dignitaries; this row curved round what was probably a flat, roughly circular area in front of the actors' platform. It was in this space, called the orchestra and symbolically detached from the stage proper, that the chorus performed. The back wall, behind the stage, contained doors through which actors might pass; very rarely did a chorus leave or enter by this means, which would have meant crossing the stage. On each side, where the seating area terminated, there was an open passage by which the chorus or actors might enter and exit. One direction conventionally led toward a harbor or the sea—Athens' own port, Piraeus, was at some distance from the city—while the other was imagined as heading inland. In the *Cyclops*, for example, Odysseus would have entered and exited on the harbor side, while the Cyclops, who arrives from the wilds where he has been hunting, would have used the other ramp or gangway. When he attempts, later in the play, to visit his brothers, he probably sets out in this same direction.[6]

The differentiation between the space of the chorus and that of the actors bears a relationship to the structure of Greek drama. Typically, the chorus did not intervene directly in the action, and their role, insofar as the plot was concerned, was largely limited to commentary. Hence, they often seem, to the modern viewer, hesitant or passive, as when the chorus of old men in Aeschylus' *Agamemnon* debate whether to rush into the palace when they hear the outcry of their king. In the *Cyclops*, Euripides turns this characteristic of the chorus to advantage, when he has the chorus of satyrs dither and make excuses for not entering the Cyclops' cave—represented by the central door at the back of the stage—and helping Odysseus blind the monster. Euripides wants the satyrs to appear cowardly; in this way too, perhaps, he sends up the protocol as it functions in tragedy, where playwrights—Euripides included—had to work to preserve the dignity of a do-nothing company of onlookers.

The chorus' chief function in drama, whether tragedy, comedy, or satyr play, was to sing and dance (the word *orchestra* literally means dancing place) in the interludes between the dramatic episodes involving the actors proper. When they had to speak as an individual, in conversation with a regular character in the play, they were normally represented by one of their number, who was the leader. Spoken dialogue was in verse, but of a kind that was, like the Shakespearean iambic pentameter, relatively compatible with ordinary speech. Choral song, however, was metrically more complex and always accompanied

---

6. On the Greek theater, see J. R. Green, *Theatre in Ancient Society* (London: Routledge, 1994).

by dance steps that were probably executed in unison. On occasion, an actor might sing antiphonally with the chorus (as the drunken Cyclops does at one point in our play) or even interrupt their song at the end of a stanza with a line of dialogue. If the action of the play had reached a delicate point at which silence was required, a playwright might exploit the occasion by having the actor try to hush the chorus, always in vain, of course. For a chorus had no alternative but to sing. In the *Cyclops*, Odysseus comes out of the giant's cave, where the besotted monster is sleeping, to scold the satyrs for their noisy chanting, which threatens to wake Polyphemus. What else were they to do, with the stage momentarily empty, if not perform a choral interlude? Once again, we have a spoof on tragic convention, which is perfectly at home in the parodic atmosphere of the satyr play. In the same way Papageno, in Mozart's opera *The Magic Flute*, lends a comic touch by being obliged to sing with a padlock on his mouth.

We have said that there were three actors who played all the speaking parts. Hence, there could be a maximum of three speaking characters on stage at any one time. In the more complex tragedies, which had several speaking roles, the actors had to change costume between scenes in order to play different characters, or sometimes make a quick change, within a scene by exiting and entering through one of the stage doors. The *Cyclops* has only three characters apart from the chorus (the chorus leader, as we have said, functions as a fourth speaker) — Odysseus, Cyclops himself, and Silenus, the satyrs' father and fellow slave. Thus, each actor would have had a single role: the lead actor, called the protagonist, no doubt played Odysseus, while the deuteragonist and tritagonist took the parts of Cyclops and Silenus. These same actors, of course, had played tragic characters in the three tragedies by Euripides — whatever they were — that preceded his satyr play on this occasion.

The actors in the Greek theater could change parts so easily because — in addition to their costumes, which could be very lavish, depending on the generosity of the producer — they wore masks: tragic masks in tragedy, comic masks in comedy, and satyr-play masks in this kind of drama. The masks were largely stereotyped, and indicated at a glance the kind of role that was being played. The masks of the satyrs, for example, were probably more or less similar from one satyr play to another, though no doubt the mask makers could introduce variations and nuances of their own. Vase paintings from a later period give some idea of what these grotesque masks would have looked like. Silenus' mask would have resembled that of the chorus, only it would have been suitable to an older and more decrepit individual. The mask of

the Cyclops was monstrous and had only one eye. Odysseus' mask, and
those of his men, who were played by silent extras, will have been
human in appearance, like tragic masks, though perhaps with some
exaggeration in the features appropriate to the farcical nature of the
genre.

Little is known about the acting style of ancient drama. The plays
do not come accompanied by stage directions, save for a very few mar-
ginal notes (there is one such direction in the *Cyclops*). Thus one is
obliged to infer from sparse external evidence and the plays themselves
how lines were delivered and what kinds of gestures accompanied
them. It is likely, but not absolutely certain, that the action was far
more stylized than in the modern theater—more akin to operatic performances, for example. The actors, who were invariably male, presumably adapted their voices to the parts assigned them, rendering them
more high-pitched when they played women, for example, although
this too is conjectural. They were performing in an open-air theater
that was the size of a small athletic stadium, and would have had to
project their voices to the bleachers. Correspondingly, all the action
on stage was imagined as taking place out of doors. That is in part why
the Cyclops' gory meal, which occurs inside the cave, cannot be directly represented; it is instead reported at length by Odysseus to the
chorus, who have been waiting outside in the orchestra. Odysseus here
assumes the role of the messenger in tragedy, a stock figure created to
narrate offstage events. Because he has to recount to the audience what
has happened indoors, Odysseus must himself be outside the cave, at
least temporarily. This puts a strain on his status as captive, and Euripides again makes the best of it by having Odysseus remark openly on
his escape, and then, in a gesture of loyalty to his comrades still within,
deliberately return in order to rescue them. Thus, dramatic necessity
is exploited in the service of characterization. Another reason why the
Cyclops' act of cannibalism occurs offstage is that brutal slayings of this
sort were not usually represented directly in the Athenian theater, but
were reserved by preference for a thrilling messenger speech.

Once all three tetralogies were over, judges (who were appointed by
lot) voted prizes for the best set of plays and the best actor. The com-
petitive ethos penetrated almost every activity in ancient Greece, from
war to oratory to poetry (compare the contest between Aeschylus and
Euripides staged in Aristophanes' comedy, *The Frogs*). Within the
plays, too, there were often paired speeches in which two characters
squared off against one another like opponents in a courtroom (Odysseus and the Cyclops debate the ethics of hospitality versus cannibalism
in this formal manner), or else a line-for-line alternation between speak-

ers. And then, when the awards were announced and the festival was ended, the season was over until the next dramatic festival with its entries for that new competition. In the fifth century B.C., that is, from the time of Aeschylus' earliest productions to the deaths of Euripides and Sophocles, a given tetralogy would normally be mounted just once on state occasions in Athens, without the possibility of a repeat performance. True, there were dramatic shows at local village fiestas in the countryside, where plays might be presented a second time, maybe in a reduced or modified form. Perhaps with such rural exhibitions in mind, the dramatists preserved their scripts, even though there was no prospect of a revival at the Great Dionysia or the Lenaean festival. In the fourth century, the works of the great tragedians were put on again, posthumously, and in time acquired sufficient prestige to be copied out officially for the state archive. From there, authorized editions made it to the library of Alexandria and elsewhere, whence a selection, including the *Cyclops* of Euripides, survived in Byzantine copies and, after the fall of Byzantium, in Italian libraries and elsewhere until the coming of print rescued them from the constant threat of disappearance.

III. THE STORY

Euripides based the plot of his *Cyclops* on the famous version of the story recounted in Book 9 of Homer's *Odyssey*, in which Odysseus, having arrived, ten years after the end of the Trojan War, at the land of a civilized people called Phaeacians, relates to his princely hosts the narrative of his wanderings (the full tale of his woes continues until Book 12). Odysseus begins his story with a brief account of a raid on a shore-dwelling population called the Cicones, where he and his men slay the natives and carry off their cattle. Here, Odysseus acquires a special vintage of wine from a priest of Apollo named Maron, whose life he spares (this wine will become important in the episode involving the Cyclopes). As they dawdle over their plunder, Odysseus and his sailors are attacked by local reinforcements (who arrive from the interior) and barely escape on their ships after suffering heavy losses. Odysseus' ships are blown off course in a storm, and their next stop is in a more fantastic place, the so-called land of the lotus-eaters, a people who feed on a narcotic plant that rids them of all thought for the future or the past. After this, they put in at an uninhabited island that lies opposite the territory of the Cyclopes.

Curiosity drives Odysseus to explore the facing shore, where he discovers, just as he does in Euripides' satyr play, the empty cave of a giant, stocked with cheeses and animals too young to pasture; the major difference is that, at this point in the account in the *Odyssey*, there are no satyrs. Odysseus' men urge him to carry off what he can to the ships and make a break for it. Odysseus, in retrospect, recognizes that this would indeed have been sensible, but he determines to await the return of the monster in order to see whether he can extract still greater gifts from him. Odysseus' motives are hardly altogether benign; he is as much a plunderer as the Cyclops will prove to be (Polyphemus himself suspects as much), although he is less savage in that he abstains from eating the carcasses of his victims and contents himself with pillaging their cattle and other provisions. Euripides, we may remark, has sanitized the hero; his Odysseus offers to pay for his provender from the beginning, without thought of theft.

Once Homer's Cyclops returns home, he proceeds directly to the business of his dinner, having imprisoned Odysseus and his men within the cave by means of a great slab of stone placed over the entrance. Odysseus, far from helpless against the giant, is on the point of stabbing him with his sword when he realizes that if he does so, he will be trapped inside. Odysseus then conceives the plan of getting the Cyclops drunk on Maron's wine and grinding out his eye with a stake, expertly hewn as a carpenter would trim a ship's mast. For good measure, Odysseus conceals his identity under the phony name of No-man, a ruse that immediately serves him well when, after the blinding, Polyphemus' brother Cyclopes come running in response to his cries of pain. It is they, rather than the satyrs as in Euripides' play, who answer in all seriousness that if no man is harming him, then Polyphemus must pray to his father Poseidon for relief from his god-sent agony. As his last trick, Odysseus fastens his men and himself beneath the Cyclops' rams, and they escape from the den as the monster lets his animals out to pasture. From there, he and his men return to their ship.

The contest between Odysseus and Polyphemus, then, is not really one of righteousness versus savagery, though the Cyclops' violation of the conventions of hospitality, not to mention his barbarous appetite, convict him of more than human viciousness. Basically, Odysseus is smart, and the Cyclops is big, mean, and dumb, though in his pastoral manner of life and his confidence in the earth's spontaneous bounty he breathes a kind of primitive simplicity: half caveman and half throwback to a bountiful Golden Age. Odysseus triumphs by his wits over the raw brawn of the giant, and this contrast is given point through Odysseus' ruse in dubbing himself No-man. Briefly, the Greek for no or not is *ou*, which appears in English as *u* in *u*-topia (noplace); the pronoun one or someone, in turn, is *tis*. Hence Odysseus christens himself *Outis* (No-one). There is, however, a second form of the word not, used mainly in hypothetical clauses: this is *mê*. When Polyphemus says that Outis has wounded him, the other Cyclopes, misunderstanding the name, naturally reply that if—note the hypothetical conjunction—*mê tis* (no one) is at fault, then they cannot be of help. However, *mêtis*, read as one word rather than two, is the standard Greek term for *cunning*, and, in the form *polumêtis* (very wily) is one of Odysseus' standard epithets. So it is cunning, the Cyclopes affirm in an unwitting pun, that has brought their brother low.

Once safely on his ship, Odysseus reasserts his true identity: he is not a nobody after all, though he might have seemed such in the Cyclops' cave; rather, he is Odysseus of Ithaca, son of Laertes. But this boast will cost him heavily, not just because of the huge boulders that Polyphemus, guided by the sound of Odysseus' voice, tosses at the ship, nearly sinking it, but also because of the curse that the Cyclops utters in prayer to his father, Poseidon, that Odysseus (for now he knows his name and can aim his imprecation) should reach home after long years and the loss of all his men, only to find his house beset with tribulations. Poseidon gives his assent. This grim prophecy and its consequences are condensed, in the conclusion to Euripides' satyr play, into two-and-a-half brief verses, and thus haven't the resonance that they do in Homer's *Odyssey*. To a Greek audience, Homeric epic was as familiar as a nursery tale, and they would have filled in the denouement unconsciously. Heather McHugh has chosen to flesh out the Cyclops' curtain-closing taunt in Euripides' version in order to restore to the monster something of the fearsome dignity that is his even in defeat.

For the story of Dionysus' capture by pirates (mentioned in the opening verses of the play), Euripides drew upon one of the so-called Homeric Hymns, that is, poems in honor of various of the gods composed in a hexameter verse that closely resembles that of the epics—though most of the hymns originated (in all likelihood) a century or more afterwards. The seventh hymn, dedicated to Dionysus, recounts how the god, disguised as a handsome young man, was abducted by Etruscan pirates who planned to hold him for ransom. The silver shackles drop spontaneously from his hands and feet, but the brigands (apart from their pilot) are not discouraged by this sign and force the god on board. Once at sea, vines sprout from the mast, a lion and a bear materialize fore and midships, and the sailors in a panic leap overboard and are transformed into dolphins—save for the pious pilot, whom the god pities and makes prosperous.

Euripides takes advantage of this episode to explain why the satyrs, who are normally in the company of Dionysus, find themselves separated from him and in captivity on this occasion: They had set out in pursuit of their kidnapped god but were shipwrecked on the Aetna side of Sicily, where the Cyclopes dwell. For the duration of the play, they are helpless—estranged from the magical power that Dionysus displays so terrifyingly on the pirate ship—and they depend for their rescue entirely on Odysseus and his men. But the god is, nevertheless, on the scene and active in the form of the wine with which he is identified—to the Cyclops' amused surprise since he finds it absurd that a divinity should choose to reside in a wineskin. In a sense, then, Dionysus does deliver his goatish slaves—by rendering the Cyclops blind drunk—but only when his brew (that is, the god himself) is administered by a human being who is not totally addicted to it.

IV. INTERPRETATION

Commentators have, in general, described Euripides' version of the Cyclops story as a minimal adaptation of the Homeric narrative, adjusted for performance on stage—Odysseus must be able to get out of the cave, for example, since the classical Greek theater did not enact indoor scenes—and adjusted as well to allow a role for Silenus and the satyrs, who had to be spliced into the tale, however implausibly, in conformity with the conventions of the satyr play. The basic armature of the episode, however, was presumed to have survived these changes intact.

A closer examination reveals, however, that the shift from the essentially two-person story of the *Odyssey*, in which Odysseus outwits the burly but bird-brained monster who has cornered him, to a three-way narrative structure that incorporates the satyrs has a deep effect on the tale and transforms the roles or functions of all the players. In place of Homer's polar opposition between Odysseus and the Cyclops, Euripides offers a ternary pattern: two extremes mediated by a middle term. Let us begin with Euripides' Cyclops: He is brutal and violent, but he is hardly a savage. On the contrary, he speaks and thinks like a sophisticated egoist, in the manner of those self-centered freethinkers whom Plato's Socrates liked to stump with his dialectic—Thrasymachus in the first book of Plato's *Republic*, for example, or the cynical Callicles in the *Gorgias*. In Euripides' time, some of the itinerant teachers known nowadays as sophists as well as other subversive intellectuals drew a sharp distinction between human convention and the laws of nature: Nature, they held, tolerated aggression of any kind in the service of one's appetites, provided one was strong and smart enough to get away with it. Human law was just a ruse on the part of the weak to tame the powerful. So Polyphemus ridicules human legislation as needlessly complicating our lives, rejects the gods' authority with flippant braggadocio, strips nature of all intentionality and responsiveness to justice, and reveres nothing apart from his own belly. This Cyclops is not so much primitive as decadent.

The satyrs, by contrast, are peaceful types, given to partying, and desolate in captivity. Whereas the Cyclopes are in general loners, each dwelling in his own cave with little use for one another, the satyrs are just the reverse: They are sociable creatures, and their role as chorus neatly symbolizes their primitive solidarity as they speak with a single voice and express themselves indifferently as "I" or "we" (this is standard practice for Greek choruses in any genre). Theirs is the community of booze, egos merged in drunken ecstasy. They are likable enough, but wholly unreliable and irresponsible. Fun-loving cowards like these are of no use when it comes to fighting, even in their own interest. They prefer to stand by while Odysseus takes the risks, without the foresight to realize that their own freedom is at stake.

In their collective devotion to festivity, the satyrs seem to be the diametric opposite of the dour and doughty Cyclops, who lives for himself alone; but extremes have a way of meeting, and the Cyclops shares some fundamental traits with the goat-men. Once he is inebriated, for example, he becomes gregarious enough and seeks out the company of his brother Cyclopes, eager to share his wine and dance for joy with them. Odysseus' problem at this stage of the action is precisely how to keep the beast at home and contain his sudden enthusiasm for good fellowship. Meantime, just as Odysseus is on the point of blinding the monster, the satyrs seem to lose their common identity as chorus and speak severally, each coming up with a different excuse for why he can't participate in the action. Despite their propensity to merrymaking and pack life, the satyrs are as selfish as they come, out for themselves first and last. In particular, Silenus, their father, is a nasty old coot, ready to sell the Cyclops' wares for a sip of wine and to lie through his teeth when the giant returns to his cave; he is even prepared, one surmises from a reckless oath he swears, to sell his own children down the river if it will save his skin.

The chief differences between the satyrs and the Cyclopes seem to reside in their dissimilar diets and the disparity in their physical strength. Polyphemus has the confidence of his toughness and will eat humans when he has the chance. It is noteworthy, however, that he does not consume satyr meat. That is, I think, another connection between the two species: They do not cannibalize each other. The satyrs, by contrast, are timid, though by no means humble. What they eat is a mystery, though they clearly find the Cyclopes' anthropophagy horrible and disgusting. They are, however, deeply dedicated to drink.

Set off against this codependent dyad of bully and crybaby is Odysseus, who is, one may recall, the only human actor on the stage (along with the silent extras who play his mates). Whereas the beast-men, both the Cyclopes and the satyrs, are supremely selfish and materialistic, thinking of nothing beyond their immediate carnal urges, Odysseus is quite civilized and humane—more so, to our lights at least, than his Homeric avatar. Right from his first entrance, he announces his intention of purchasing provisions honestly, without a hint that he might plunder others' goods (this is a comic turn as buying and selling have no place in tragedy). Then, in his exchange with Silenus, he asks whether the Cyclopes have cities and government and whether they respect strangers—as he himself presumably does or would. The absence of civic life leads Odysseus to inquire whether human beings or wild animals inhabit the land, to which Silenus replies ambiguously: "Cyclopes," insinuating that they are neither the one nor the other. Nor are they—any more than the satyrs themselves are. The uncertain species status of the Cyclopes raises, indeed, an interesting puzzle: If they are not human, then neither are they cannibals for eating men, any more than lions are or humans who consume cattle. After all, the Cyclopes do not feast on one another, nor, as we have seen, do they include satyrs in their cuisine. To the extent that they are other, then, they are no worse than carnivores. The Cyclopes are a strange hybrid: They speak and think and this is enough to qualify them as human (especially to a Greek) and to make their culinary habits abominable; yet they, like the satyrs, are of a different race. This conundrum is a reminder that the monstrous is precisely that which defies classification rather than that which is violent or hideous by nature.

To return to Odysseus, not only does he reveal himself as law abiding with respect to trade or exchange of goods, he is also a model of loyalty to his men. When he finds himself outside the Cyclops' cave—as he must, since the constraints of Greek theatrical conventions (we have said) did not permit interiors to be shown—he declares aloud that he could save himself, if he chose, but that would be an injustice to his friends. Odysseus lives by a code of reciprocity and fairness, whether in regard to commerce or allegiance to his subordinates—and in his relations, we may suppose, with guests as well. In this he differs from the Cyclops and the satyrs alike. Where they are self-centered and given only to consuming, not to conferring in return, Odysseus both gives and takes: The satisfaction of his needs is matched by his generosity. Thus, Odysseus—or humanity in general—is the necessary third term between the egoistic isolationism of the Cyclops and the collapse of self represented by the satyrs: He stands for interconnectedness, which mediates between extreme individualism and the sameness of the horde.

If the extremes represented by the satyrs and the Cyclops tend to meet, however, in a common voracity and narrow devotion to pleasure, how can Odysseus' sense of mutuality mediate between them? What comes first, it seems, is the human idea of relatedness, which presupposes termini that are distinct yet united. One can destroy a relationship between two things either by cutting the cord that joins them, as it were—thus converting the endpoints into independent monads like the Cyclopes—or collapsing the extremes together into a single mass: This is the undifferentiated unity of the mob. This is a very abstract way of talking about Euripides' *Cyclops*, of course; it is offered merely as a diagram or simplification of the complex social behaviors that operate within the play.

To take another set of differences among the personalities in the *Cyclops*, Odysseus is the only character who does not drink wine in the course of the action. Not that he is a teetotaler, of course; he has no objection to drinking wine when it is appropriate to do so. But he knows how to do so in moderation and is capable of exercising self-control, in particular in the difficult circumstances in which he finds himself in the Cyclopes' territory. Neither Silenus nor Polyphemus exhibits a comparable restraint. Further, both the Cyclops and the satyrs have an inordinate interest in sex. Polyphemus threatens to rape old Silenus; the chorus of satyrs draw a lubricious inference from the Greeks' recovery of Helen, imagining that her liberators must have taken turns screwing her. Odysseus, in this play, has no time for such monkey business. He is in perfect control of his appetites.

I do not want to convert Euripides' Odysseus into a Boy Scout, although his impassioned defense of the Trojan War as a fight to preserve the gods' shrines and keep the Greek world safe and free rings of juvenile patriotism. It is not as though the Trojans had attacked Greece, after all. (Granted, Odysseus is striking a pose in his attempt to sway Polyphemus.) What is more, Odysseus himself had a seamy family history, according to an account that is alluded to by Silenus, which made him the son or grandson of the thieving Sisyphus rather than of Laertes, as in the *Odyssey*. Human beings undoubtedly come off as superior to Cyclopes and satyrs in this play, but Euripides, with the impartial calumny of satire, also undercuts their pretensions to transcendent virtue.

While the date of the *Cyclops* is unknown (metrical and stylistic features suggest a time late in Euripides' career, but this method of dating is insecure, particularly for a satyr play, since this is the only complete one we have), it certainly coincided with the period of Athens' imperial hegemony, and very likely with the Peloponnesian War, the great conflict between the Athenian and Spartan confederacies that dragged on over the last third of the fifth century B.C. In the year 415 B.C., the Athenians launched a huge armada with the intention of reducing Syracuse, the chief city on the island of Sicily, and bringing the western sea under its control, thereby choking off Sparta and its allies. It is tempting to see an allusion to this expedition or its aftermath in Odysseus' encounter with the monster who resides beneath Mount Aetna, but there is little in the play that suggests political allegory. It is safer to suppose that Odysseus' participation in the campaign at Troy, and the justifications he offers for it, smack of Athenian imperialism in a general way, and that the Cyclops may not be wholly fatuous or out of character when he derides the war as a hideous waste of life for the sake of one faithless woman. Again, Polyphemus' dark prophecy at the end, muted though it is in the original, may have resonated, however subtly, with fears or memories of Athenian naval disasters in distant parts.

Finally, what of the gods? The Cyclops believes he himself is one, and descended from another, Poseidon; the satyrs and their father Silenus are the constant companions of Dionysus. Odysseus is only a mortal, but he claims to have protected the gods' rites and temples, the means, that is, by which humans render unto the gods what is their due and receive from them in turn aid and sustenance. In his two prayers for the gods' favor, Odysseus makes clear their obligation to deal justly with mankind in return for the worship that is given them; if they fail their part of the bargain, then there remains no reason for human reverence or faith. Here again, we see the code of reciprocity that governs and defines human conduct in all domains. For all its spirit of caricature and travesty, Euripides' *Cyclops*, and perhaps the satyr play in general, offers an optimistic vision of human ties — as opposed to raw nature — that can hold its own against the somber universe of tragedy.[7]

V. STYLE AND TRANSLATION

The *Cyclops*, like all classical Greek drama, is written in verse. It is thus poetry, albeit in a less elevated register than the great choruses of

7. For interpretations of the *Cyclops*, see William Arrowsmith, "Introduction" to his translation of the *Cyclops*, in David Grene and Richmond Lattimore, eds., *The Complete Greek Tragedies* (Chicago: University of Chicago Press, 1956); Robert G. Ussher, "The *Cyclops* of Euripides," *Greece and Rome*, n.s., 18 (1971) 166–79; David Konstan, "Euripides' *Kyklōps*," in John J. Winkler and Froma Zeitlin, eds., *Nothing to Do with Dionysus?* (Princeton: Princeton University Press, 1990) 207–27.

Aeschylean tragedy and similarly sublime lyrics. Most of the lines are in the verse characteristic of dialogue, which contains six iambic beats in three pairs of two beats each; marked breaks in the line (caesuras) tend to fall within a foot, rather than between feet, to prevent the line from collapsing into its parts. The iambs are not constituted of unstressed and stressed syllables, as in the English iambic pentameter, but rather of short and long syllables, an effect unfamiliar in English verse but which we are attuned to hear in songs. Besides straight dialogue, there are also choral odes, but in the *Cyclops* these are few and brief. The odes, which were accompanied by an oboelike instrument and sung rather than recited, had complex metrical patterns based on rather free combinations of longs and shorts, something like the lines of varying length and rhythm that make up Wordsworth's *Ode on Intimations of Immortality*. Vocabulary and, in one detail, pronunciation too (a broad, Doric *a* in place of *e* in certain word forms) distinguished the choruses from spoken verse.

The diction of the *Cyclops* is in general less grandiose than that of tragedy, admitting more colloquialisms and witty turns of speech, but it never loses a stateliness in language and syntax that it shares with the higher genres of Greek poetry. Anyone who reads ancient Greek can tell in a moment that this is not prose, even apart from the fact of meter; the comic effects in the play, in turn, do not rely mainly on violations of linguistic decorum. Euripides does vary the tone and style for humor's sake, but it is done subtly rather than in a spirit of verbal slapstick.

For this translation, Heather McHugh relied in the first instance (as she explains in her foreword) on David Kovacs' version (1994) in the Loeb Classical Library series (which the reader may confidently consult for a literal prose rendition of the original) in combination with other translations; but the result resembles only accidentally, when at all, any of the versions with which she worked. I contributed clarifications of some particular points of exegesis (we do not always follow Kovacs' text, for example), and a few suggestions on phrasing. I was thrilled when Heather elected to adopt a couple of them.

I can assure the reader that the present translation is faithful to the original. I mean faithful first of all in the literal sense, that is, the translator honestly reproduces the meaning of the Greek text, passage for passage, rather than bending it to an interpretation of her own. Here and there, especially in the choral songs, which cannot withstand word-for-word conversion, Heather has permitted herself slightly greater liberties. A few times, for example in the wordplay on numbers in the prologue and in the Cyclops' final prophecy, she has expanded on hints or possibilities in the original in order to give more bite to the English version. None of this obscures the significance of the Greek, and it will not mislead the reader as to the import of Euripides' text. Such changes as Heather made are, in my view, in the service of a second and higher kind of fidelity, which is to the poetry of the Greek. One can be faithful to this only by rendering it into English poetry, and what is more, poetry that can be read aloud, and on the stage. The present translation is for the ear as much as for the eye. It is Euripides in English, and I hope that those who hold the book in their hands may also have the pleasure one day of seeing the play performed in the theater.

DAVID KONSTAN

TRANSLATOR'S FOREWORD

It would be hard to miss one fundamental metaphor in any story involving disreputable giants: The one giving rise to the question what, in any sense that matters, makes a mortal being big. For it is the Cyclops' own sense of engorged self that Odysseus must topple in the course of the action. And this giant's dimensions are constantly materialized in the play by reference to the size of the meals or drinking vessels he requires or how many men would be needed to drive the sharpened tree into his eye. Like any great poet's details, these narrative particulars are not without significance in the moral field of the story. Polyphemus is the son of the geosphere and his self-centered universe has a single moon-eye. Insofar as Number One is all he's looking out for, he's the perfect figure of the global consumer, mere amounting's profanation of the very *art* of numbers, the very essence of magnanimity. And when, in that moment of doubt every great figure experiences at its nadir, Odysseus fears that the greatest One might not come to his aid, his dread is of an emptiness at the heart of the most transcendent numbers: Zeus may be nothing but a zero.

I've emphasized the numbers-play throughout the dramatic play because numbers afford us such a fertile field for cultivating questions of value. Luckily for the comic registers of the play, there's something not only vile but also preposterous about the value systems of Silenus and his sons: Silenus is introduced melodramatically enumerating the sufferings he's endured in the service of Dionysus. (The satyr's mimicry of the epic sufferings of Odysseus, whose traveler's travails are the very stuff of epic figures, is only one of the play's many mirrorings.) I've emphasized this satyr-element by stylizing the ludicrousness in Silenus' self-pity-as-self-promotion: He contradicts himself, even as he counts off his agonistic accomplishments—for with each enumeration of his sufferings, he claims that they're innumerable. By foregrounding this tallying of countlessness, I hoped comically to activate the rhetorical equivalent of a moral motif, one that might help prepare the audience for what will later crop up not only in Silenus' own effusions (see lines 264–73, in which Silenus so overplays his betraying hand, and also 293–99, where he swears by too much to be true) but also in the the prolix language of the chorus (Silenus' sons), whose long-winded hyperspecifications about how precisely to be of service turn out to be precisely self-serving. The chorus gives us to understand how a word like *consideration* might have come to mean mere *compensation*. All their big words are to little ends, as a sufficient dilation on action amounts to an evasion of it.

This is just one trail of emphases I've highlit for figurative contrast, a contrast between the circles of the richest human relation and the zeros of mere accumulation, of social and spiritual indifference. Silenus claims that he loves his sons "more than anything on earth"—but offers *their* lives as collateral, not his own. And when the sons hear of that, they damn their father. By contrast, the circle of faith to which Odysseus pays homage very much comprehends the circle of family loyalty (which he defends when Silenus insults Odysseus' father, Sisyphus; and which he invokes in alluding to the Cyclops' filial relation to Poseidon). And insofar as Odysseus is NOT merely self-interested, his concerns extend beyond those of his own family. Indeed the largest interests to which he alludes include the interests of civility, a principle that would admit to its realm and benefits even the Cyclops, were the creature to honor family (see lines 321–33), or honor the community of mortal moral code (lines 334–38). Odysseus finally appeals to the Cyclops on the Cyclops' own grounds: All these social sympathies may ultimately benefit the individual, whereas self-interest unrefreshed by communal empathy ends up incurring its own demise.

But the Cyclops' circles of authority are empty, involving as they do the evacuable rounds of the belly, the wheel of seasons without will, and gaping holes in human law. (The zeros of the legal nooses and loopholes to which he alludes will seem familiar to contemporary audiences.) The Cyclops (who himself is named for circularities of vision) thus becomes the foil for the more transcendent circles of Zeus. In the lineage of storytellers, Odysseus is kin to the playwright himself, a "no one" who knows much, and who is in fact the grounding figure. Unlike the chorus, Odysseus weaves a story not for sensational or voyeuristic ends, but to elicit human sympathy, greatening human action beyond the spheres of merely local identity. Some time after Euripides, medieval theologians will propose for divinity the circle whose center is everywhere and whose circumference is nowhere, its boundaries beyond all mortal ken. This construction of divinity's circle is close kin to Odysseus' ringing, concentrifying senses of relation.

Silenus and his sons are, by comparison, the moral relativists. Expedient, they are the sneakiest things afoot. Their idea of poetic license is opportunistic, and when the balance of power swings from one figure to another, they change their footwork to save their skins. They want to be part of the big triumph, they dream of fame—but when the mortally dangerous, morally decisive act looms, they bog down in questions of critical one-upmanship: Whose hand should be first on the weapon, whose hand number two? So they evade the act itself. At times they seem to represent the decline of servile nature into mere aestheticism: Given the chance, they set themselves up as the music critics of the singing Cyclops, so that ultimately even their consternation seems trivial, in view of the brutalities the Cyclops has committed. Where Silenus and his sons could be said to be doubletalkers, forked of tongue, Polyphemus speaks in only one tongue, and the one tongue says there's no god bigger than himself. When Odysseus tries to address Polyphemus' sense of honor and human community, Silenus tells the Cyclops to ignore him: The only fat you should chew with him, he says, is his own. Have his tongue for dessert, and then in how many voices you'll speak!

But Odysseus is a world traveler. If he speaks in many tongues, it is as often for establishing a mutuality as it is for selfish guile or guise. So the question of numbers is the question of language as well: How can one represent oneself without duplicity? La Rochefoucauld's acid *aperçu* (that the function of language is to conceal our thoughts) smacks of Silenian intercourse. Self-service is intimate with duplicity. A self-serving nature is by nature a slave (and when circumstances release the chorus from one slavery, it looks forward to another, as the play's last line suggests). The chorus toadies up to whatever power seems likeliest at the moment to afford a reprieve. Odysseus is, by contrast, the figure of nobility, and nobility (it needs repeating, in the context of America's distaste for even its own aristocratic histories) does not impose the hierarchies of order—it *incurs* them. The great man knows there is always something greater than himself.

The selfish man, however well fed, is the small man: He thinks of nothing beyond his own circle of interests. The Cyclops with his overfed emptiness, his diminished firsts, his fattened fists, his infinite regress of an eye trained only on itself, has something in common with Silenus. But Silenus stands on slipperier ground. The Cyclops stands, at least, on a single solid mortifying philosophical ground; by comparison the members of the chorus seem all the more detestable as they hold no premises undesertable.

Of course, all these figures seem reprehensible in comparison with the figure of Odysseus as he appears in this play, where he makes, even to the Cyclops, civilized appeals on moral and ethical grounds, and promises to save even the traitorous Silenus and his sons. But Euripides does not oversimplify Odysseus' virtues. The Greek audience would come to the play knowing the *Odyssey*'s history of plunderings and subterfuge; and with good reason Homer refers to Odysseus as Polytropos, man of many turns, man of many tropes. When Polytropos meets Polyphemus, we have a metamyth: a meeting of the figures of figures.[1]

And in this play the field of character *resemblances* is exploited as fruitfully as is the field of *distinctions*. For example, the argument—in lines 316–92—between Odysseus' version of a life of traditional honor and the Cyclops' version of a life of self-satisfaction finds its mirror-image in the later responsorial between Odysseus-as-entrapper and a rather endearingly drunken Cyclops. Here the positions of honor are reversed: Odysseus has to deceive the Cyclops in order to avenge his companions. (Honorable necessity, like honorable men, is submitted to hierarchical patterns.) And when the Cyclops proposes in his sentimental wallowing a sort of love, that is, he puts forth the virtues of sharing some wine with his brother Cyclopes down the road, he has to be dissuaded of this virtuous impulse by Odysseus, who steers him back toward more selfish grounds (lines 594–97):

> CYCLOPS: I'd like to give my brothers some of this stuff.

> ODYSSEUS: You keep it to yourself, and they'll admire you more.

> CYCLOPS: But giving it, I'd be a better brother.

> ODYSSEUS: The best of revelers wind up in fisticuffs.

1. Interesting to consider, in this connection, the early seventeenth-century grammar play, the *Heteroclitanomalonomia*, based on Andrea Guarna's *Bellum Grammaticale*, in which parts of speech are personified, and engage in warfare. Indeed, another play from the same period, the *Gigantomachia*, equips its giants with the weapons of whole hills—which they heave at foes, as does Euripides' Cyclops—and then calls those hills a grammarian's "heteroclites" (the Indo-European root, in its suffixed form, is *klei-tor*, "incline, hill"). I do the ancient dramatist the homage of assuming that (since his audience would have come to the performance equipped with a rich foreknowledge of the stories) he might well enjoy not only the play *of* the fable, but the play *with* it.

Here Odysseus becomes the legalistic hairsplitter and noose-looper: In order to serve the larger justice, he has to commit an injustice. In consequence, a civilized reader finds himself sometimes sympathizing with the monster, whose cries of pain and betrayal will soon be derided by both Chorus and Odysseus, commoner and nobleman alike.

The world's worth cannot be weighed according to numerical inci-dence — numbers of people per usual unit or type — whether the type is of nation or decade or color or faith. American democracy pays lip service to this largest principle, but there's another principle we find our natures less well equipped to sponsor. The majority will not always be just. And if one has to be *like* to be liked, sooner or later one has (like Silenus) to lie: One cannot always resemble without dissembling. Odysseus' strength of character shines out most forcefully when he finds he stands alone.

As I say, I've emphasized a number of numbers in my rendition of the play, in an effort to counterpose the footwork of fancy (poetry and pleasure, the Bacchic virtues) against its mimicry in the fancy footwork of evasion and unreliability; the number one of the logos against the number one of self-interest; the sphere of moral nourishment versus the zero of empty self-satisfaction or godlessness; and so on. The gist of the numbers-play, it seems to me, remains of use today, to those of us who live in latter-day versions of the very democracy to which Odys-seus first alludes when he arrives in Cyclopsland. Its gist is this: The man who carries within himself a sense of the cumulative value (not additive progress) of human history; the man aware of the depth of his relationship to other living beings (including beasts); the man aware that family relations and the relations of myth are similarly "telling"; the man aware of his subordination before the orders of nature and god; and, finally, the man aware of the ultimate insufficiency of any one group-interest or self-interest — that man achieves greatness. His richest holding is insight. No other material greatness will matter, no other carnal accounting can count.

Thus can poetry count. I've replicated no accentual or syllabic fea-tures of the Greek original, but I have tried to recognize affinities within word-strings, echo-effects, and emanations (sound-trails, image-contrails) that are the very stuff of poetic configuration. Some of my early efforts to raise to the surface the "round eye" etymologically pres-ent in the word *Cyclops*, or more conspicuously to apply inside the poetry the many-storied etymology of Polyphemus, were ultimately re-linquished in the course of making this translation. Where I have kept some stubborn fidelity to the linguistic freight of the original is where song-shapes were called for or where words repeated themselves for poetic purposes. The chorus abuses its brutes in brutish language (48–68); and the beasts and their keepers alike are subordinate to an *Über*-brute. Insofar as the Cyclops is the god of his underworld, his hierarchy is the mirror image of Odysseus' godly one. And if at the end I'm tempted to emphasize the inverse orders of Polyphemus' mephitic domain, his stubborn conviction that by digging deeper in, he can come out on top, perhaps that spiritual topography will concatenate with the end of the *Inferno*, where it's hard to know which way is up until the reader emerges again out of the world of fable and into that of his own life's story.

At the play's outset, the Cyclops was said to be out "tramping the wilds," but the audience soon discovers to what extent Polyphemus harbors the wilderness inside himself: Civility is carried in the single soul. It's not achieved by the superaddition of mere numbers of people. A city can be a wilderness, as in our day we know too well. In the mock-civilization of which the Cyclops is the emperor, he becomes also the very figure of spoiled refinement. To the extent that Polyphemus is a delectator and gourmand who might be recognizable to American audiences, I felt entitled to update some of the references (availing myself, for example, of certain polycultural culinary registers; it never hurts when a hint at the eater lurks within the eaten, like a Gorgon in the Gorgonzola). The figure of corrupt or self-absorbed wealth is satirically registered in the passages in which Polyphemus mulls over his meals—in lines 245–46, for example, where he might as well be the orderer of adjectives in a Seattle cappuccino-line (is it no accident Seattle's best anagram is "let's eat"?)—or later, in lines 277–81, where he savors the competing claims on his prandial imagination: how much to have of roasted man, how much of braised.

It's clear from very early on that Silenus and his kin are of a different herd than is Odysseus: Indeed, there's a closer kinship among the sheep, the chorus, Silenus, and the Cyclops than there is between any of them and Odysseus. (Odysseus' ruses in other stories of his travels, his thefts of provision, his infidelities to family, are not featured in the Euripidean *Cyclops*.) Here Odysseus is, among all the characters, the one most prepared to sacrifice himself for something bigger than himself. Even the uppermost figure in any human order (and perhaps especially that figure) must acknowledge an order greater than its own; and until the spheres of relationships are seen to radiate toward and comprehend the uncontainable, no man's figure is of value, and Zeus's zero threatens to be one more empty Cyclops eye: means without meaning.

The eye that matters, of course, is the mind's eye, eye of empathetic imagination. Even when Odysseus is free from the cave, he can't stop seeing the plight of his friends and so is driven by imagination (the mind's eye) to return to their aid. By contrast, the chorus solicits prurient details about the rape of Helen and all the sensational particulars of the torments of Odysseus' friends (as something sufficiently bestial in contemporary folk is drawn to highway carnage or the most predatory particulars of the dirty-movie channel). The chorus does not possess the solitary eye of the Cyclops: theirs is the compound eye of the voyeur. Moral blindness has everything to do with the action of this play.

The Cyclops, if Silenus' own testimonies are to be believed, has never before been known to revel. Yet when the intoxicated creature bursts into song, Silenus mocks the rural oaf who never took singing lessons. Silenus savages the Cyclops not for his savagery, but for his want of singing skill — his lack of taste — and so manages less to distinguish himself from, than to resemble, the Cyclops (who fancies himself a sort of culinary connoisseur, as cannibalistic characters go). Silenus would enlighten the Cyclops only to lord it *over* him: wants first for the lout to "see the lyric light," and then wants both his lights put out — of sight and song alike.

At the dramatically crucial moment, when the chorus members give their last-minute (lame!) excuses for not helping Odysseus (I think I'm suffering from leg cramps, I think I've got a sprain), America's colloquial application of "I think" seemed to me to be opportune: far from securing, it makes insecure. For despite the human presumption to distinguish itself from all lower orders by virtue of its intellect, and despite the elaborate word-works of the chorus' excuses, these guys aren't so much turning things over in mind as they are turning tail. To the enlightenment that really counts, a 20–20 vision can be blind. What matters most is visible by insight.

I shouldn't leave David Konstan with the sole burden of explaining the liberties I've taken at the end of the play. The abruptness of Euripides' ending was the most dramatically frustrating element of the play for me, as a literary artist. In Kovacs' literal version, the Cyclops ends by saying: "Oh no you won't: I shall break off a piece of this crag, hurl it, and crush you, companions and all, to bits. I'm going up to the hilltop, blind though I am, by climbing through my tunnel." Then the chorus ends the play by proclaiming, as if it had not heard the Cyclops' threat: "As for us, we shall be shipmates with Odysseus and ever after serve in Dionysus' train." And that's that. An entire drama has been predicated on the suspense of our wish to know whether or not the Cyclops would prevail over his guests, and we wind up with only these three last turns in the dialogue: Odysseus saying "Now we'll escape"; the Cyclops saying "No you won't"; and the chorus saying "Now we are saved." By way of culminating dramatic sequence, that one (in and of itself) strikes me as fatally inconsequential.

Euripides is no fool. He could count on something we can't count on now. A contemporary audience may not know the Cyclops episode takes place early in Odysseus' journey home; indeed, it's likely to know nothing of the story of Odysseus at all. The Greek audience, acquainted with the myths revisited in this play's performance, knew the Cyclops wouldn't kill Odysseus, yet also knew Odysseus was wrong to think his sufferings were all behind him. That's why I felt I had to compensate for the dramatic incommensurability of my audience with the Greek one—somehow, for the drama's sake, fill in some of the story's once-implicit play of mutualities, to serve Euripides' ends today.

Odysseus has just revealed himself to have a flaw, after all: He dismisses the blinded Cyclops just at the moment the creature acknowledges that "There was a story to the effect that you would cause me this suffering—but in that story you went on to suffer." This is a crucial point, it seems to me. The telling of stories has all along been coded into Polytropos' name (man of many turns and tropes) and into Polyphemus' name (the many-storied, often-spoken-of, much-famed). These names are earnable only after notable deeds take place: So there's a delicious anachronism (and metanarration) at work in the Greek drama. And it is Polyphemus, not the polytropic Odysseus, who recalls to the audience that fact—the fact of foretelling's force, and memory's. But this reminder of the power of the story is dismissed by Odysseus. He thinks he has already put behind him the narrative of his suffering. That's the pride preceding a fall. Odysseus may mock the Cyclops, but in fact the Cyclops is seeing clearly for once in his life, and at this moment Odysseus seems the blinder one. In a sense, he wants to pre-empt history all by himself, turn into mere *fait accompli* the ever-unwinding fable of past and forecast. Such a disposition is of moment for dysmemoried America.

> CYCLOPS There was an ancient prophesy that said
> I would be blinded by you, in this way.
> It also prophesied a punishment for you:
> to roam around the sea for what
> would seem an endless age.
>
> ODYSSEUS So now you are a sage. I say the future you
> predict

> is history already. Take all your time warps
>   and your prophesies,
> and go to blazes. I, for one, am going to the
>   beach.
> A boat awaits, to take us home
> from this infernal Sicily.

CYCLOPS Oh no, you don't. I'll break this rock apart
> and throw down boulders, till your boat and
>   you
> and all your friends are smithereens.
> I may be blind, but you are all at sea —
> I may be single-minded: you are all adrift.
> You think a son of earth was what you
>   dropped —
> but I'm Poseidon's son as well, and I can lift.
> You twisted time to your own ends —
> but I can still negotiate a twisted space:
> I'll feel my way to Nomen's land. My
>   blindness
> knows its place: it has no boundaries, it
>   doesn't stop.

And only then did I return to what literally occurs as the Cyclops' last line in Euripides's text:

> I'll take an under-tunnel to the mountaintop.

Not only the Cyclops' darkness, but the chorus's self-absorption won't be stopping, either. Unlike the Cyclops, the chorus has suffered no rebuke, and no enlightening. It continues with characteristic sweeping statement and unreliability, blind faith in itself and its day:

CHORUS LEADER Forget his malices and miseries. What future
> could so big a blindness tell? His selfishness
> is ancient history. Whereas, now, we —
> we are the model of modernity — that's why
> we're saved: to multiply, at last, in luxury!
> By change's wind and by the future's wave,
> let's sail, O brave Odysseus!

> Just forward us to Bacchus, and
> we'll be the best of slaves.

That snap into fast-forward, to escape ambiguous questions (such as those the Cyclops has raised about time's telling and retellings) is a familiar chronic mechanism. There's a blindly buoyant cheerfulness about the chorus' evasions, a turning away from all but the moment's most convenient histories and ends; it may ring a bell for Americans who chance to see this play. As I write at the end of the twentieth century, most of my fellow citizens (for all their investment in education) have at best a dim familiarity with the venerable stories of human history. Even a great civilization may wind up deepening its moat: Its security in its own premises becomes a form of provinciality. The insular condition isn't only rural Sicily's. I hope my modest embellishments at the end of the play supply for such an audience some of the links and bridging that Euripides' audience would have assumed from the popular legacy of fable.

To those who would admonish my audacity, I submit by way of exculpatory evidence the literary quality of the result in English. The second life of poetry, says Eugenio Montale, is memory. And if ancient poetry is to be taken to heart by new worlds of English-speaking consumers, the first obligation of the translator is to its memorability as English poetry. It was in the first place only with trepidation that I accepted Oxford's challenge to create yet another version of Euripides' *Cyclops*—a poet's version abetted (and not restricted) by the scholar's understandings. The very thought of identifying—and then hashing out—questions of poetic interpretation, negotiating the resources and limitations of two languages at once, is enough to daunt any sensible soul. On my own, I had done translations from the French (a language I knew well); and I had collaborated with my husband in translations from the Bulgarian and German (languages as Greek to me as Greek is). Comparing the products of my solitary enterprises with those of the collaborations made it apparent how much is possible if you are conversant with, and confident of, your consultant's gifts. Most important is the capacity richly to read poetic turns of mind wherever they occur, in source and target languages alike—for the greatest of all translatorial paradoxes is this: So few native speakers of ANY language speak Poetese.

Just as rural islanders off Maine and Norway and Chile may have more in common with each other than with inland citizens of their own nations' capitals, poets everywhere may be more perversely versatile, more diction-addicted, more word-working, and more language-loving than even the most knowledgeable other readers and writers. Artists everywhere may be uncannily alert to perceptual patterns, image-grids, sound-systems, frames and flows of relation: and indeed there were times in collaborative translation when I could intuit (from patterns in the raw material of the literal versions I was supplied) image-thoughts or figural ideas my collaborator may at first not even have noticed—despite his being the native speaker or scholar in the source language—but later confirmed. It's a translatorial truism that one cannot hope to duplicate in another language the precise music or sense-shades of the original; but it's less often observed, and no less important, how rarely native speakers of the target language imagine the ranges of musics and means, spare or sumptuous, the spirit of a poem might require. Of my competence in the sensual and syntactical resources of the English language I am as confident as I am of the scholarly skills, literary instincts, and collaborative understanding of David Konstan, to whose remedying astuteness my first drafts were submitted. To be consigned to such auspices proved most reassuring: For fine scholarship requires more than one kind of vision, and Konstan's insights were compounded at once of authority and of grace.

There were two other overwhelming inducements to accept the project. One was the sudden appearance just then, by chance, in my readerly purview, of an inspiring translation from the ancient Greek—Seamus Heaney's version of *Philoctetes* (a book Heaney calls "THE CURE OF TROY"). To read it was to be reminded (with that rush of thrill one feels at an old knowledge reinvigorated) how livening an act of interpretation can be. Heaney's *Philoctetes*—with its glimpses of human being in the act of being (and even not being!) itself, feeling (and even not feeling!) itself—amounts to a lovely rereading of the old drama: a resuscitation of identity's ancient social senses, inside a contemporary reader's ever-perishing self-senses. The poetic intelligence with which Heaney approached the already long-known *Philoctetes* gave me heart: for great literature is new again and again, in each reader's acts of best attention. And a translation is not a review, nor is it the same view from a different angle: It is, in fact, a new view.

The *Cyclops* itself I'd known through translations (including the most literal prose versions) already available: First and foremost, the authoritative groundwork of David Kovacs' *Cyclops* in the Loeb Classical Library series (published by Harvard). On this version (considered by most scholars to be the most dependable literal rendering in English) I relied most heavily—with gratitude for the Greek *en face* and critical notes throughout. I was also notably served, as the work proceeded, by an extraordinary resource: the on-line Perseus Project. Accessible on internet instruments not even dreamt of a few years ago, it seems, for classical studies, already a hermeneutic indispensability. It's hard to overstate the delight one feels (literally! at one's fingertips!) on double-clicking any word in the Greek play, and finding oneself zoomed straight to the comprehensive reference, a collation of some of the best classics authorities in the world. Not only the scholars but also the universities that collaborate to administer the Perseus Project deserve high praises for their service to the students and standards of Greek and Roman literary studies.

But it is first and finally Euripides—with all the life still in him—who most irresistibly tempted me to venture forth, despite my remove from the grounding Greek, on a careful rendition of his satyr play (the only complete extant satyr play!)—and to do so with all the fierce affections of my own inheritance and readership, the American momentum of my love of language in general, and of poetry in particular. The *Cyclops* you see here was written with an English-speaking audience—perhaps especially an American audience—in mind. I've adjusted the colloquial tones and comic registers to provoke that audience in ways I hope are consonant with the satyr-play's own raucous origins. The Cyclops who, on his island of *ipse*, appears as a connoisseur of carnal indulgence, an apologist for modern self-gratification, broken off from the old-world chain of faith and family, is a timeless figure (and so can seem American to an American): He's a skeptic about "piety and empty sentiment"; he sees the rule of law as no more than a noosework of loopholes. More reflexive than reflective, oriented more to logistics than to the logos, he can be found in contemporary life making his solitary rounds in a cell-phoned Lexus. . . .

One of the ancient masters is said to have said: "Let other men praise ancient times. I am glad I was born in these." It is just as blind to think of Greek and Roman cultures as originary as it is to think of our own as ultimate. Perhaps we're too fond of the human narrative we've made so emphatically our own, the one we imagine will end in our own time: Perhaps we have not imagined some of the eternities in which human souls might yet survive. But what a contemporary Polyphemus has in his head to love, he has in his life to lose: for we lose our selves, having each but one. The grossness of the single Cyclops, and the meanness of the collective chorus, mustn't make contemporary audiences shrug "We're not like those old cannibals and cowards." The people we are blindest to, inevitably, anatomically, are we. It is ourselves, therefore, the greatest poets stage.

We're no less villains at our worst than are Silenus with his tribe or Cyclops in his greedy solitude; and no more heroes at our best than is

Odysseus, always accompanied, and always alone, in his own ways. He wasn't always just, and wasn't always true, but kept the two ambitions simultaneously alive, in the circuit of a single human gaze. Imagination's greatest contract is with the universal moral insight: "one's all" must be doubly understood. As of yet—this writing, this millennium—the mind's eye isn't guttered out.

Seattle   HEATHER McHUGH
April 1999

CYCLOPS

CHARACTERS

SILENUS companion of Dionysus

CHORUS satyrs, sons of Silenus

ODYSSEUS King of Ithaca

POLYPHEMUS a Cyclops

ODYSSEUS' SHIPMATES (silent parts)

Line numbers in the right-hand margin of the text refer to the English translation only, and the Notes on the text at p. 69 are keyed to these lines. The bracketed line numbers in the running head lines refer to the Greek text.

SILENUS O Dionysus, do you know
how many times—not only now
but since I was a youth—I put myself
through agonies for you? So many times
they're numberless. Number one: that time
the jealous goddess Hera made you crazy,
and you strayed away from home, away from all
your mountain nymphs and nannies—and I
went after you. Innumerable labors! Labor number two:

when you were battling to protect   10
Olympus from the geosphere's gigantic sons,
and I was there beside you, shield in one hand,
spear in the other, goring that enormous Enceladus
dead, right through his armor! (Wait a minute,
am I spinning fables as I speak? By Jove,
I'm not! I swear I shared
the war-spoils with you later.)

And Dionysus, here I am today, suffering more than ever.
The torments can't be counted. Torment number three:
when Hera riled those pirates out of Tuscany: they seized
      you   20
for their slave trade overseas, and I got wind of it. We
      took to sail,
my own sons manning oars on either side, while I stood
      tiller. Lord,
how high and low we looked for you! We whipped the
      gray sea white!

But rounding Cape Malea we were cast
by a bad east wind upon this Aetna headland.

37

Living in the nearby caverns—last not least—
were Cyclopes: Numberless Horror Number Four,
Poseidon's lawless sons. One-eyed, but with a thousand
stories to his name, Polyphemus is known abroad
for his uncommon fondnesses for men: 30
he eats them raw.

And he's the one who keeps us here as slaves, my sons
          and me,
who meant to save *your* skin from slavery. So I, Silenus,
and my family, instead of being wined and dined,
must tend this faithless creature's flocks. My young
must raise the young of sheep, there on the hillsides;
here my labors take a more domestic form:
to swill and sweep, make ready for his meals.
And now if you'll excuse me—work is work—
I have to rake this floor before   40
the one-eyed one gets home.

          Enter at Ramp A the CHORUS OF SATYRS, *driving sheep.*

But wait—those are my sons approaching with their
          flocks.
Hello, my boys! How lively is your step!—one *two*, one
          two—
the same, it seems to me, as back in our old salad days,
when you and Bacchus partied all the way
to sweet Althaea's house, in lyric
choreography, instead of lack-lust chores.

CHORUS   (*to a recalcitrant ram*)

Where do you think you're going,
you son of a high-class dam? What path
do you think you are taking there?—it goes   50
to the crags. Have you eyes in your head?
Can't you see how much better this breezy way is,
to the green? There's a meal and a river-wave
there at the cave-mouth, all of your little ones
bleating in bed—

come on, now, git! Over here to the slaphappy slopes
of home sweet home! Git on now! Git this minute! or
be got by me, with the help of a stone. You, there!
you horny old head of the household—get a move on!
You're supposed to be guardian of guardians,   60
top dog in the Cyclops sheepfold, for as long
as he's out trekking in the wild.

                                                    (*to a ewe*)

That goes for you too, sweetie—get
those mammaries on home! it's time you were nursing
your young in that cave. The little bleaters
slept like lambs all day but now they're missing you.
Come on! Get in! Give up your Aetna meadows
and enjoy this nice big pen.

Alas for me, this barnyard's
far from Dionysian—not a wine-god to be found,   70
no dancing, no amazing wands or holy ecstasies,
no drums or fountainheads of youth, no wineskin's savor.
Not a single mountain Nymph with whom
to strike up drinking songs
for the goddess Aphrodite. Ah,

how fast we chased the god of love in the good old days,
I and my lady-friends, so fleet on their white-hot feet! . . .
Dear Dionysus, where are you without us?
Tossing your golden hair for nobody? while I,
who was your happy servant, serve the worse for exile,   80
wearing nothing but these awful skins,
and missing your fine company,
a man-slave at the mercy of

some giant one-eyed misbegotten thing . . .

SILENUS Be quiet, my sons! Get inside quickly, with the animals!

CHORUS LEADER   (*to the attendants*)

You heard him! Move it!

39

They and the animals enter the cave.

But, father, what's the hurry?

SILENUS I see a ship on the beach down there! It's Greek!
Yes, those are sailors coming toward our cave
with someone who appears to be their captain.   90
They've got some empty sacks about their necks,
presumably for food; and pails for water.
O unlucky visitors! Who could they be?
They can't imagine what Polyphemus is like, or just
how inhospitable this ground is, where they disembark;
they haven't got a clue what bad luck brought their trip
to Cyclops territory, where a man is made a meal—
but not the way he wants. Now you be quiet, and we'll
    learn
exactly where these men are from, who land at Aetna's
    very lip . . .

Enter at Ramp B ODYSSEUS *with his men.*

ODYSSEUS Strangers, can you show us to a drinking stream?   100
Our thirst is killing us. Or tell us who might sell
provisions to my starving crew?
                              By God, it seems
we've happened on a Bacchanalia! I see
a festival of Satyrs near the cave. I'll greet
the eldest first. Hello, there, venerable one!

SILENUS I greet you, stranger, in return. But tell me
what's your name, and nation.

ODYSSEUS I am the lord of Cephallene, from Ithaca. My name's
Odysseus.

SILENUS   (*aside*)

I've heard of this guy—he's a sponger if I ever saw one!
Son of Sisyphus, the famous pusher.   110

ODYSSEUS I am the son of Sisyphus—but spare us the aspersions.

40

SILENUS Where did you sail from, to end up in Sicily?

ODYSSEUS From Ilium, and from the war in Troy.

SILENUS What happened, couldn't find your way home?

ODYSSEUS I am here because a windstorm overpowered me.

SILENUS Ill winds! The very devils that did me in!

ODYSSEUS So you were forced ashore as well?

SILENUS I was chasing pirates who had kidnapped Dionysus.

ODYSSEUS What's this country? Tell me who its people are.

SILENUS This place is Aetna, highest mountaintop in Sicily.   120

ODYSSEUS But where are all the city walls and fortresses?

SILENUS There is no city. This is not a place of men.

ODYSSEUS What then? Wild animals?

SILENUS In a manner of speaking. They are Cyclopes,
        and take to caves, not houses.

ODYSSEUS Who's their king? Or is it a democracy?

SILENUS It's each man by and for himself. There is no
        government.

ODYSSEUS Is Demeter respected here? I mean,
        do they plant grain? What do they live on?

SILENUS Curds and whey and sheepflesh, sir.   130

ODYSSEUS And are they friends of Dionysus? lovers of a good
        retsina?

SILENUS Not a chance. No dancing goes on here.

41

ODYSSEUS Do they at least love gods, and welcome strangers?

SILENUS Strangers are their favorite appetizer.

ODYSSEUS Surely you aren't saying that they *eat* them?

SILENUS Every man who's set foot here since us.

ODYSSEUS This local Cyclops, at the moment,
just where is he? Over there in his abode?

SILENUS He's off on Aetna with his hounds, to hunt for game.

ODYSSEUS You've got to help us get away. You know what you can
do?   140

SILENUS Not yet. I bet you'll tell me.
What I can, I will.

ODYSSEUS Just sell us bread—we haven't got a single crust.

SILENUS I told you, we have nothing here but lamb.

ODYSSEUS A lamb chop wouldn't hurt a human hunger.

SILENUS There's also milk, and cheese.

ODYSSEUS Well, daytime is the right time for a business deal.
Give us a look at the inventory.

SILENUS Tell me, first, just how much gold you said you had?

ODYSSEUS It isn't gold we carry, but the wealth of Dionysus: we
have wine.   150

SILENUS You've got some wine with you? That's just
what we've missed most! Best news in a blue moon!

ODYSSEUS It was Maron, son of the wine-god himself, who gave it to
me.

42

SILENUS You're telling me you got your wine from the child I
                   cradled in my arms?

ODYSSEUS I mean from Bacchus' own child, if saying so will mean
                    my meaning's any plainer.

SILENUS Now, about this wine, is it still on the ship out there,
                   or here with you?

                                        ODYSSEUS *takes out the wineskin.*

ODYSSEUS: Right here, old man! A wineskin full of it, before your
                     eyes.

SILENUS That's barely a gulp, by my standards.   160

ODYSSEUS I dare you to drink this wineskin dry, you and your whole
                    entourage.

SILENUS Is there some magic way to make
                   more wine flow in?

ODYSSEUS I'll say—and twice the volume that flows out.

SILENUS Now that sounds like the fountain of *my* youth!

ODYSSEUS Perhaps you'd like to taste a bit before . . .

SILENUS I would indeed! A touch is halfway to a handshake.

                                        ODYSSEUS *brings out a drinking bowl.*

ODYSSEUS Look, I've even brought the stemware.

SILENUS Holy Dionysus, give me some—I can hardly remember
                   what it's like to wet my lips.   170

ODYSSEUS Your wish is my command.

SILENUS   (*sniffing*)

         O my! O my! A fine bouquet!

43

ODYSSEUS So there's a wedding in the works?

SILENUS Not yet—but I can smell
some serious deflowering to come.

ODYSSEUS *hands him the cup.*

ODYSSEUS Indulge, then—take a taste. A praise
should never smack of empty words.

SILENUS Oo whee! Oo whee! I think the god of wine has just
invited me to dance! O lay! O lay!

ODYSSEUS It goes down nicely, doesn't it?   180

SILENUS Right to the toenail-tips!

ODYSSEUS We'll pay you too, of course.

SILENUS Just keep the red stuff flowing, we'll forget the gold.

ODYSSEUS Then you bring out the lamb and gorgonzola.

SILENUS Yes, indeed I will, my master can be damned.
I'd give his many flocks for just one cupful
of this wine—I'm dying for a topflight lowbrow
tippler's kind of time, a little jump off lovers' leap
in old Leucadia, a good long bob there in the brine.
The man who doesn't love a drink has got a few   190

screws loose: one swig and look! your stick stands up,
your hand gets deep in cleavage and you start
the breaststroke toward her burning bush,
you're dancing with the Nereids, nary a care
in the world. I could *kiss* a drink like this!
To hell with the Cyclops! Tell him where to put it—

head up his bumhole, and mud in his eye!

Exit SILENUS *into the cave.*

CHORUS LEADER Listen here, Odysseus. We've got to have a little talk.

ODYSSEUS Of course, since we are such fast friends.

CHORUS LEADER Did you really take Troy, and then take Helen too?   200

ODYSSEUS We laid waste to the whole of Priam's house.

CHORUS LEADER And tell us, once you had the girl, did you take turns
                with her?—
            the traitoress, craving such multitudes beyond her mate!
            One look at all those fancy breeches, foreign colors,
            gold around his neck, and she was in a fever,
            sure as sin, and hapless Menelaus left behind,
            poor man. Ah, womankind! I say
            let *all* of them go down—
            and preferably on *me*!

                        Enter SILENUS *from the cave.*

            And here you go, my lord Odysseus—   210
            the tenderest of lambs, a flock of them;
            plus cheeses in abundance, made of finest milk.
            They're yours. But now you've got
            to leave, and quickly—only first
            I need a little more to drink.
                    Uh-oh! Somebody's coming!
                        It's the Cyclops! God, what should we do?

ODYSSEUS If what you say is true, there'll be a big to-do,
            and then we're done for. Where's a place to hide?

SILENUS Inside the cave, and quick—in there you can't be seen.   220

ODYSSEUS A dangerous idea, I think, to fly into a cage.

SILENUS Don't worry—there are many nooks and crannies in
            there.

ODYSSEUS I won't do it. All of Troy would turn in its grave if I ran
            from just one man, after standing up with shield in hand
            against so many. If I must die, I'll do it nobly;
            and if I live, I'll have my reputation.

45

Enter at Ramp A, *the* CYCLOPS

CYCLOPS Make room! Get out of my way! What's happening here?
Or maybe I should say, what *isn't* happening? You, boy,
standing around so underemployed, is this your idea
of a Dionysian holiday? Can't say I notice   230
any evidence of your beloved Bacchus in the area,
don't hear his drums and castinets. How are my lambs?
Are all the newborns nursing? Is the milk put up
in curdling buckets yet? Somebody answer me!
I have a club that soon enough will raise
a hue and cry, if you do not.
Look up, not down,

when I am speaking to you!

CHORUS LEADER   (*looking up at Polyphemus*)

I'm looking up! My head is turned toward God himself
and all his starry retinue—by God, I think I see Orion!   240

CYCLOPS But have you got my dinner ready yet?

CHORUS LEADER There's something very to your taste, in fact.

CYCLOPS And milk in mugs?

CHORUS LEADER Milk by the barrelful, if you desire.

CYCLOPS Cows' milk or sheep? Or maybe for today
some exquisite blend of the two?

CHORUS LEADER Anything you say—just don't take any slugs of me.

CYCLOPS Don't flatter yourself. All that fancy
footwork in my belly? It would be my death.
Now, wait a minute!—who are all those people near my
         cave?   250
Did pirates come ashore? And why are my lambs outside,
         tied up
with willow-ropes—my cheese-bins strewn about—

46

what's going on? Who's that old baldie there,
the swelled-up one, so red in the face you'd think
he came here straight from battle?

SILENUS Ooo! Ooo! the pain! the pain!
I'm feverish from taking all those punches.

CYCLOPS What punches? Who would beat you up, old man?
You certainly look the worse for wear.

SILENUS These men, my lord—attacked me when I tried   260
to stop them robbing your own lordship blind.

CYCLOPS But don't they know I am a god,
from gods descended? How could they dare?

SILENUS I said the same thing, but it didn't stop their
plundering—
they even pinched your best cheese, though I fought
them
valiantly, in vain. And then they started carrying
off your sheep. They said they'd leash you too,
like any ugly dog, and under your own eye

they'd cut your guts out, lash your back with whips,
and then tie you up completely, hand and foot, and
throw you   270
into the darkest dungeon of their ship, and then . . . and
then
they'd sell you for somebody's heavy labor, or maybe it
was
make you do their millwork somewhere . . .

CYCLOPS You don't say. (To SILENUS) You there! On the double!
Sharpen up
my carving knives and get a good blaze going on the
hearth.
(SILENUS *makes a movement toward the cave*) I'll slaughter
these offenders
in a flash, and have my fill of them. I think I'll serve one
up
as barbecue, straight off the coals; the others should be

delicately braised—for tenderness's sake. I've had
too many mountain meals—enough of lions,   280
deer and such. It's far too long since I enjoyed a man.

SILENUS   After so much ordinary venison, my lord, variety is
                  pleasant.
                  Indeed, it's quite a while since we had guests for dinner.

ODYSSEUS   Polyphemus, hear out your visitors. We left our ship
                  only to ask where we could buy some food. This man of
                         yours,
                  after a drop of wine, decided he would sell us all these
                         sheep
                  for just one cup. He was a willing businessman—
                  we didn't twist his arm. You can't believe a word he says;
                  he's covering his *own* malfeasances, now that he's caught
                  red-handed, selling goods of yours without authority.   290

SILENUS   Are you accusing me? Then I say go to hell.

ODYSSEUS   I'll go to hell if I am lying.

SILENUS   O Cyclops, I will swear by your own father, great
                  Poseidon,
                  by the venerable Nereus and Triton, by Calypso, by
                         Nereus'
                  good daughters, by the holy oceanful and all the fishes in
                         it,
                  dearest master, sweetest master, o most handsome
                         Cyclops, I would never
                  sell your private property to men. If I am lying, let my
                         sons
                  (whom more than anything on earth I love)
                  themselves be damned to hell.

CHORUS LEADER   Be damned *yourself*! I saw you selling food to them!   300
                  If I am lying, let my father rot! Don't blame the strangers.

CYCLOPS   (*to the* CHORUS *leader*):

                  And why should I take *your* low word for it? I've trusted
                  this Silenus more

48

than any judge on Judgment Day. I won't believe he's
    lying now.
But still, I'd like some answers from you foreigners:
Where are you from? Where is your homeland?
What's your native town?

ODYSSEUS We're Ithacan by birth. We sailed here after sacking Troy,
when we were blown off course by storms.

CYCLOPS So you're the ones who went to punish Ilium
for kidnapping that good-for-nothing, Helen?   310

ODYSSEUS We are the very ones who did
endure those awful wars.

CYCLOPS What a disgraceful mission!
Sailing all that way to Phrygia
for just one worthless whore!

ODYSSEUS It was a god's design: don't blame us mortals for it.
You, who are yourself a noble sea-god's son,
we beg you: do not kill in mere cold blood
such men of innocent goodwill, who merely chanced
upon your house. Don't make a godless meal of us.   320
All over Greece we kept your father's temples
sacred: there at Taenarum his harbor's
perfectly secure; safe are his caves
at Cape Malea, sound is Sunium,
Athena's holy ground, and rocks
still glitter with the silver there.
Wherever we have gone
Poseidon rules.

The real disgrace would be
if we'd surrendered to the Trojans   330
all these Greek possessions. In a sense,
we fought for you—who (living here at Aetna,
where a rock can flow like fire) are living in the farthest
    reach of Greece.

But if these points don't move you, take to heart
the universal law of men: a shipwrecked stranger must

49

be treated kindly, given gifts of hospitality and clothes,
instead of being turned like beef on spits, to bloat
a rude host's belly. Priam's land has treated us already
to an orgy of bereavement, too many men were speared,
and too much blood drunk up by battlefields. Too many
    wives   340
made widows, too many gray-haired parents sent on
childless to their graves. If you wolf down today what's left
    of us,
to whom can anybody turn for help? I beg you, Cyclops,
put aside mere gluttony, and call upon your godlier re-
    serves:
unholy self-indulgence will, in the long run, hurt you
    most of all.

SILENUS Here's my advice, Polyphemus: don't chew the fat
with the likes of him, that is, unless the fat you chew
is his. I wouldn't let a bit of him be wasted, sir, if I were
    you.
And after every delicacy's done, and finally you put his
    tongue
into your mouth, just think how many tongues you'll
    speak in, then,   350
preeminent Polyphemus, and all of them as eloquent as
    his.

CYCLOPS I'm quite fed up, but not quite fed,
my puny little visitors. You ought to keep
a fact or two in mind: the wise man worships
no god more than wealth, and its self-satisfactions:
all the rest is so much piety and empty sentiment.
As for the headlands of my father's seaside temples,
I live well enough without them. Why throw them
into your argument? Of Zeus' flaming anger, I don't fear
a lick: I don't believe he's any more a god   360
than I am. He won't worry my hereafters.
Let me tell you why.

Whenever he sends down his storms, I find my shelter
in a well-sealed cave, I dine on roasted calf,
I lie there belly-up and satisfied, I drink
a whole damn milk-vat dry, and then

I drum on the resounding tub until
the sound drowns out his thunder.

As for fierce north winds and snow, I wrap myself
in warmest suede and fur, I bank the blazing fire,   370
no cold can bother me. My animals are fed all season
on the grass the summer lavishes on us
whether it wishes to or not. I dedicate
my profits all to me—and not to any far-off god:
I sacrifice the best of everything to this: my belly.
Show me a bigger divinity! Simply to eat and drink,
day in day out, to give oneself no pain—
in the eyes of any sensible man

that's all the Zeus that matters.
As for senators and lawyers, turning the world   380
into a noose of cleverness and net
of complications, I say let them
hang themselves in their own loopholes! I will not
deny my heart's delight. And at the moment,
it would be my heart's delight
to eat you up. You'll get
some presents from me, sure enough—
a nice big fire to warm you, and a lot of sea-salt
sent with father's compliments, a good bronze pot
to keep you toasty warm. Now I suggest   390
you go inside my cave, and pay your homage
to the god who dwells within—

and soon we'll add your ego to his altar.

ODYSSEUS God, have I escaped the tribulations of the Trojan War,
and all the gales at sea, only to wash up here at last,
where nothing holy can be harbored in a heart?
Athena, Zeus' daughter, help me now! My danger
is too great for words. O Zeus above, the guardian of
              guests,
whose home appears so bright up there among the stars,
look kindly on our low condition! If you don't watch over
              us,   400
who worshiped you so many years,
you're more a Zero than a Zeus.

The CYCLOPS *herds* ODYSSEUS *and his men*
into the cave. SILENUS *follows.*

CHORUS O Cyclops, you may open up
the gaping gateworks of your throat,
and baste and braise and broil and roast
the devil from your guests—
and then recline in fleeces, the better
to rip and rend and tear and taste
the morsels of their flesh—

but leave me out of it. I want no share.   410
You fill your vessels as you will. I say
someone should do away with this unholy house!
Away with all its self-indulgence, greed and godlessness!
Away with any cruelty that treats
itself to other creatures' torture, or
a refugee to nothing more
than the rotisserie. . . .

Enter ODYSSEUS *from the cave, distraught.*

ODYSSEUS My God, what can a human being say
in the face of a horror story come to life—
I'd never have imagined I would see,   420
in mortal form or time, such searing
inhumanity. . . .

CHORUS LEADER Odysseus, what are you saying?
Surely he hasn't already consumed
one of your beloved shipmates?

ODYSSEUS He has indeed—he looked to find,
and hefted in his hands,
the plumpest two
of all our company.

CHORUS LEADER Poor souls! But tell me every last detail.   430

ODYSSEUS We got into his cavern where he heaped the fire with
hardwood,
logs enough to load three wagons easily, and then

52

he set the kettle on the fire to boil. Near by the fire
he spread the ground with fir boughs, for a bed;
then milked the cows till he'd filled to the brim
a ninety-gallon tank, and next to that he set
a cup of ivywood—it must have measured
more than four feet, rim to rim,
and six feet to the bottom.

Next he set to whittling spits   440
of buckthorn, burnt the ends
and scraped them with a blade.
When all was done to the satisfaction of
the cook from Hell, he grabbed my friends.
He cut the first man's throat with one
quick swipe, and drained his blood
into the cauldron; then he seized
the second by the foot, and dashed
his brains out on a rock. He cut them up
with an atrocious knife, and roasted   450
all the fleshy parts upon the fire;
the arms and legs he threw into the stewpot.

I stood there in my utter wretchedness, the tears
were streaming from my eyes as I was forced
to watch him work. The others cowered farther off
like swallows in the crannies of the cave, their faces
drawn and pale. And when the glutton finally fell back,
all sated with his meal and belching something foul—

I had a sudden thought, as if from heaven.

Filling a cup with Maron's wine I offered it to him: 460
I said, "O Cyclops, son of sea-gods, you should try
this drink the Greeks think so divine. A ruby cupful,
worthy of a god." His belly filled to bursting with
his execrable meal, he still took up the cup, and drank it
        down,
then raised a hand in sudden admiration. "Dearest
        friend,"
he said, "this drink is very good, on top of my good
        meal."

I saw that he took pleasure in it, so I filled the cup
    again—
I knew the wine would be his own undoing: wine
would make him pay.
                Eventually he felt
inspired to sing. I went on plying him, cup after cup,   470
amounts of wine that couldn't fail to make a stone heart
    feel
a little overwarm. And even as we speak, my crew
is sitting there in tears, while he belts forth
the discord of his songs; the cavern echoes
with the awful sound. I've managed to escape,
and wish to save us, you and me, if you should so desire.

But are you really ready now to leave the clutches of this
    brute—
to live in the Naiads' halls? Your father wants to go,
but he's so weak he's stuck to the winecup there,
a bird in lime, his flapping all in vain. But you—   480
you still are young. You could have Dionysus
for your lord—he's not the Cyclops kind.

CHORUS LEADER Dear friend, I long to see the day
when we are free from this unholy creature!
Not to mention that I've had too long
a widowed wine-spout of my own—
it needs a lick or two.

ODYSSEUS Then listen to my plan, and we can still escape.

CHORUS LEADER Believe me, I'm all ears.
There is no dulcimer I'd rather hear   490
than news of dead Polyphemus.

ODYSSEUS The Cyclops wants to take this Dionysian drink
over to the other Cyclopes, for partying.

CHORUS LEADER I get it. You want to catch him in the woods
and cut his throat, or push him off a cliff.

ODYSSEUS Not quite. I tend to work more cunningly.

CHORUS LEADER So tell us then. We've heard
                       that you are clever.

ODYSSEUS First of all, I want to keep him here. I'll tell him wine is
                    such a pleasure
              he should keep it for himself, and never share. But when
                    he falls asleep   500
              (as he will do, for Bacchus packs a wallop) then I'll take
              that olive stake I noticed in his house: it has a point
              I'll sharpen with my sword, and darken in the fire. And
                    then
              when it is good and burning, I'll remove it from the
                    flame
              and tiptoe to his very face and drive the paling
              deep into his eye. I'll melt that eye with fire,
              I swear, I'll make his mountain weep.
              The way a master carpenter applies
              a turning drill, I'll whirl
              the firebrand down   510

              into his sphere: I'll burn
              his only eyeball out.

CHORUS LEADER Hear hear! The thought of such inventions makes me
                       giddy with delight!

ODYSSEUS And after that we'll go, together with my friends, and your
                    old father
              all aboard my ship of ebony, away from this forsaken
                    land.

CHORUS LEADER Is there some way that I could help you do this
                       brilliant blinding of the Cyclops, just as men will share
                       in tributes to the gods? I want to play a part
                       in this remarkable revenge.   520

ODYSSEUS Indeed, I'll need your help: the branding-tree
              is far too big for just one man to heft.

CHORUS LEADER I'd lift a hundred wagons'-worth of torch
                       to smoke the wings and stingers from
                       that wasp nest of his eye.

ODYSSEUS Now that you know my plan, just keep it quiet.
         Once I give the word, do everything
         your master carpenter commands.

         Just being free this moment from that awful cave—
         imagine how I long to flee! But saving myself   530
         is nothing short of evil if it means
         I leave my friends in there to die.

CHORUS LEADER Now tell us, when we have our hands there
         on the firebrand, who should be first to grip it,
         who the second? Under the Cyclops' eyebrow,
         actually to grind his lights to dust, just
         how shall this huge instrument be handled?

                              Singing from inside.

         Sh! He's coming from the cavern,
         he's completely drunk—and badly out of tune, to boot.
         He ought to pay for this offense to sense, the sheer   540
         inharmony of it. Let's sing him one better,
         my boys! The lout's in need
         of lyrical enlightenment—
         without our best
         aesthetic help
         he'll soon be *doubly* blind.

              Enter the CYCLOPS *from the cave, leaning on* SILENUS.

CHORUS   The man who revels raises high
         a lusty Bacchic air,
         a vineyard breeze with which to ply
         his trades to anywhere.   550

         He dances out and round the bend
         to seek a layman's sport:
         his arm around his trusty friend
         for immoral support.

         The girl who lies upon the bed
         voluptuous and young

can make men speechless, it is said
with just a touch of tongue.

With that, and wine, he has to shine.
He'll sing—and then he'll score.   560
His rod is red, his staff divine—
just open up the door!

CYCLOPS Oh lah, oh lay, her hold is deep—
we'll drink it to the lovely lees.
My heart is skipping steps to keep
abreast of her festivities.

I'm loaded to the topdecks—sing!
Spring's in the bed, spring's in the year.
To brother Cyclopes let's bring
the cheapest gal—a gallon's cheer.   570

Come on, now, friend, give back that wineskin.

CHORUS Handsomely disposed to come
and show a wench your family jewels,
don't wait for candlelight and gloom—
a maiden's made for you to rule

in daybreak's shift, and daylight's gown.
She's dewy there, inside her nook.
But more than that will bait your hook.
(And more than that will be your crown!)

ODYSSEUS Now listen, Cyclops, as it happens   580
I know very well
this Dionysus you've been drinking.

CYCLOPS Now wait a minute—you don't mean the god's the *drink*
itself?

ODYSSEUS The very wellspring of our *joie de vivre*.

CYCLOPS Well, I belch his airs with pleasure, I'll say that.

ODYSSEUS And that's the way he likes it. He won't hurt a hair on
          anyone.

CYCLOPS But why would a god want to live in that hole?

ODYSSEUS Wherever he goes, he feels at home.

CYCLOPS No god should wear just one bare skin.

ODYSSEUS Why not, if it creates delight? You mean   590
          you don't enjoy it?

CYCLOPS Hate the skin, but love the wine.

ODYSSEUS Then drink your fill, Polyphemus. Here's to your health.

CYCLOPS I'd like to give my brothers some of this stuff.

ODYSSEUS You keep it to yourself, and they'll admire you more.

CYCLOPS But giving it, I'd be a better brother.

ODYSSEUS The best of revelers wind up in fisticuffs.

CYCLOPS They wouldn't dare. I may be drunken, but I won't be
          smashed.

ODYSSEUS My friend, a drunk should stay at home.

CYCLOPS The man who drinks without a lively crew is crazy.   600

ODYSSEUS The man who drinks within a living room is wise.

CYCLOPS What should we do, Silenus? Stay at home?

SILENUS I say we stay. Why bring more banqueters to bear?

ODYSSEUS What's more, the ground right here is flowery and soft.

SILENUS What's more, the sun right here is perfect for a draft.
         Why not lie down, and rest your bones?

The CYCLOPS *reclines.* SILENUS *puts the bowl behind him.*

CYCLOPS Hey, why put that bowl back there?

SILENUS So no one knocks it over.

CYCLOPS I know how you work—you'll drink it dry
        behind my back. I say   610
        you put it here between us.
        Stranger, tell me now

        what name you go by.

ODYSSEUS Call me No-man. In return,
        to win my thanks, what favor will you do?

CYCLOPS Of all the number of your men,
        I promise I will eat you last.

SILENUS That's a good gift, for a guest!

               SILENUS *surreptitiously helps himself to drink.*

CYCLOPS What are you doing there? Wetting your lips with the
        wine?

SILENUS Not quite. The wine has wet its lips with me: 620
        it seems to find me irresistible.

CYCLOPS You'll soon be sorry. That wine doesn't love you.

SILENUS On the contrary, I swear, it's falling for me:
        I believe it loves my inner beauty.

CYCLOPS Slave, you're here to pour, and hand the cup to me when
        it is full.

SILENUS I need to keep an eye on how the wine is doing. Just a
        little look.

CYCLOPS You're driving me entirely mad. Now hand the tankard
        over!

SILENUS Not until I've given you a crown

> (*He puts a garland on the* CYCLOPS)

and given myself a little tip as well.

CYCLOPS This wine-pourer is nothing but a cheat.   630

SILENUS This wine-pouring is nothing less than sweet.
Now wipe your mouth: here comes a swig.

CYCLOPS (*wiping his lips and beard*) All right, I'm ready.

SILENUS Tilt back on your elbow as you drink—like this.
See how I tip it up and up, so far you cannot see.

> *He drinks with head back, hidden by the cup.*

CYCLOPS Hey, what are you doing there?

SILENUS You see? Elegantly down the gullet.

CYCLOPS Stranger, I want you for my pourer.

ODYSSEUS I'm not entirely unacquainted with the stuff.

CYCLOPS So pour, already.

ODYSSEUS I am pouring. You just quiet down.   640

CYCLOPS That's not so easy when you're all tanked up.

ODYSSEUS (*handing him the bowl*) There you go:
now drink it dry! Here's looking at you! Bottoms up!
A whiner and his wine should end together.

CYCLOPS God, this grapevine is a clever sort of plant.

ODYSSEUS Drink deeply after eating well, and you'll
sleep like a baby. But leave even a single drop,
and the wine-god makes you parched.

> *The* CYCLOPS *takes a long drink.*

CYCLOPS Ahoy, ahoy! I nearly drowned in there. What pleasure I am
feeling—I see earth and heaven whirlpooling together.
There's the throne of Zeus and all his wheeling retinues!
I think I'll give them each a kiss. I'm feeling quite seduced.   650
But I'll be damned if any of those Graces gets me—not a
chance! Instead, I'll take this charmer of a Ganymede to
bed. He suits me better. Boys are always more appealing.

SILENUS Who are you talking about? Not me, I hope?

CYCLOPS Oh yes, by Zeus, from whom I'm now about
to spirit you away!

SILENUS My sons, I'm done for! This is a fate worse than death.

CYCLOPS You do not like your lovers drunk?

SILENUS By god, the taste of wine   660
is turning sour on me.

Exit the CYCLOPS, *dragging* SILENUS *into the cave.*

ODYSSEUS Come on, now, noble sons of Dionysus,
soon he'll be asleep in there, still belching from his meal.
The firebrand's waiting for us, sending smoke-signals—
there's nothing but the deed to do: burn out his bloody
eye.
Just pull yourselves together now, with all your might and
bravery.

CHORUS LEADER Our hearts are strong as iron and our will is strong as
stone.
Go quickly, or my father will end up the shafted one. We
stand prepared.

ODYSSEUS Hephaestus, rid us of this pestilence. With Aetna's
metalwork and sparks
(of which you are the god) now to your neighbor's awful
eye, apply your arts.   670
And Morpheus, o god of sleep and child of darkness, pray

61

come over him, don't leave a glimmer: blind his gaze.
Don't let Odysseus—for all his Trojan glories—
die ingloriously here, at the hands of a man-eater,

cheater of heaven. Help us, or else chance itself
will seem to be the greatest god, and heaven
just a happenstance.

Exit ODYSSEUS *into the cave.*

CHORUS Now soon the host who swallows up his guests
will feel the touch of fire-tongs at his neck,
and tongues of fire upon his shining eye.   680
The very tree he felled out of the sky
will rise again from ash, in red reaction.
A little present from the god of wine! And one good turn
of this, a turn of that, and many happy returns—until
that big black eye is blind. That way he learns
the price you have to pay, the fee
for drunken satisfaction. After that,
we're up! we're off! to ivy-covered halls
where Dionysus dwells. We'll leave behind
his single-minded self, self-centered mind—   690
and we'll be free—if there can *ever* come
a happiness from hell.

Enter ODYSSEUS *from the cave.*

ODYSSEUS For god's sake hold your tongues, you animals,
and seal your lips. I forbid you so much as to blink
or clear your throats or breathe, for fear you'll wake
the Cyclops up, before his eye is disciplined with fire.

CHORUS We're shutting up. We're swallowing our words.

ODYSSEUS Let's go inside in force, now,
stand together unforsaking.
There's a red-hot hand of poker   700
in there, ready for the taking.

CHORUS LEADER Before we go, could you explain
      exactly how we are to hold the stake
      while burning out his eye?

LEADER OF CHORUS A I think my standing too far from the door
      . would not be so effective.

LEADER OF CHORUS B I think I'm suffering from leg cramps.

LEADER OF CHORUS A I think I got a sprain myself,
      I can't think how.

ODYSSEUS You sprained your leg while standing there?

LEADER OF CHORUS A Apparently. And now there are   710
      some ashes in my eye.

ODYSSEUS My cohorts are turning to cowards.

CHORUS LEADER So it's cowardice to want to save
      my neck? to want my teeth intact?
      I'd rather be a coward then, in fact—
      for people hurt you when you're brave.

      I know an Orphic spell that I could train
      on the firebrand, till it rises of its own   720
      accord, marches to the Cyclops' skullbone—and then
      pow!—it bursts the bastard into flames.

ODYSSEUS I always thought you might be of this kind.
      It's true: you are untrue. My friends
      will be my only surety, at last,
      before this awful beast.

      And you—who find no arms to lend—
      can help with some encouragement at least.

            Exit ODYSSEUS *into the cave.*

CHORUS LEADER As long as his own mercenaries
      run our risk for us, we'll do the cheerleading. 730
      Death to the Cyclops! Let the sucker burn!

CHORUS   Hooray for heroes! Stick it to him good!
          Tighten the screws on the son of a bitch!
          Burn his lookout station down! That's right,
          that's right! incinerate the sinner! Ram your point
          straight home! Not one more guest for dinner! Atta boy,
          Odysseus! Drive it in, and pull it out, you'll turn the
                tables on
          his awful appetite. Skewer him deep, past lash and brow;
          impale his every view. But turn his lights out
          as you go: don't let him get   740
          a lash at you.

                 Enter the CYCLOPS *from the cave, his face all bloody.*

CYCLOPS   Aiii! Aiii! My eye!!! The sun is turned to cinders!

CHORUS LEADER   That's a pretty song. Sing it again
                for us, dear Cyclops, would you?

          CYCLOPS   Woe is me! I've been assaulted! Traitors!
                    Vermin! You will not escape unscathed!
                    I'll stand here in the entranceway
                    and block your passage with my arms!

CHORUS LEADER   O Clopsy-Wopsy! What's that tune you're bellowing?

          CYCLOPS   My god, without my eye, how can   750
                    I look? They've ruined me!

CHORUS LEADER   You don't look good. In fact you are
                uncommonly unsightly.

          CYCLOPS   Uncommonly uncomfortable, as well.

CHORUS LEADER   What happened, did you black out in the fireplace?

          CYCLOPS   No, by heaven! No-man did this to me!

CHORUS LEADER   So you did this to yourself?

          CYCLOPS   No, no, I tell you, No-man stabbed my eye.

CHORUS LEADER I see. You say you are not blind.

CYCLOPS Says you. I say I cannot see.

CHORUS LEADER But how could no one make you blind?   760

CYCLOPS You're making fun of me.
But where is No-man now?

CHORUS LEADER He's nowhere, as you see.

CYCLOPS That goddamn guest destroyed me
when he drowned me in his drink.

CHORUS LEADER It's true, a little port in a storm
can be a downright danger.

CYCLOPS For mercy's sake just tell me:
have the strangers left? or are they still inside?   770

CHORUS LEADER They're standing here, quite quietly,
beneath the overhang, though they are not hung over.

CYCLOPS To my left or to my right?

CHORUS LEADER Your right.

> The CYCLOPS *moves from the entranceway.*
> ODYSSEUS, *his men, and* SILENUS *slip silently out of*
> *the cave.*

CYCLOPS Where?

CHORUS LEADER Right next to the cliff. Have you got it in hand?

> The CYCLOPS *runs into the cliff.*

CYCLOPS I got it in the head. I think my brain is broken.

CHORUS LEADER I see they've made a break for it, themselves.

CYCLOPS I thought you said that they were over here.

CHORUS LEADER But I meant here.   780

CYCLOPS Where do you mean?

CHORUS LEADER This way, your left.

CYCLOPS You're mocking me again, I'm desperate
and you are toying with me.

CHORUS LEADER I'm not lying to you now, I swear. He's right in front of
you.

CYCLOPS You fiend, where on earth are you lurking?

ODYSSEUS Far enough away from you
to keep Odysseus' person safe.

CYCLOPS Odysseus, is it? So No-man has a new name.

ODYSSEUS No. But *some* man had, the day   790
my father called his son Odysseus—
he can be odious as well, if he's compelled,
as you have seen. You owe your fate completely
to your own ignoble appetites. My victories in Troy
mean nothing, if I let you get away
with murdering my friends.

CYCLOPS There was an ancient prophesy that said
I would be blinded by you, in this way.
It also prophesied a punishment for you: 800
to roam around the sea for what
would seem an endless age.

ODYSSEUS So now you are a sage. I say the future you predict
is history already. Take all your time warps and your
prophesies,
and go to blazes. I, for one, am going to the beach.
A boat awaits, to take us home
from this infernal Sicily.

Exeunt ODYSSEUS *and his men by Ramp B.*

CYCLOPS Oh no, you don't. I'll break this rock apart
and throw down boulders, till your boat and you
and all your friends are smithereens.   810
I may be blind, but you are all at sea —
I may be single-minded: you are all adrift.
You think a son of earth was what you dropped —
but I'm Poseidon's son as well, and I can lift.
You twisted time to your own ends —
but I can still negotiate a twisted space:
I'll feel my way to Nomen's land. My blindness
knows its place: it has no boundaries, it doesn't stop.
I'll take an under-tunnel to the mountaintop.

Exit CYCLOPS *into the cave.*

CHORUS LEADER Forget his malices and his miseries. What future   820
could so big a blindness tell? His selfishness
is ancient history. Whereas, now, we —
we are the model of modernity — that's why
we're saved: to multiply, at last, in luxury!

By change's wind and by the future's wave,
let's sail, O brave Odysseus!
Just forward us to Bacchus, and

we'll be the best of slaves.

Exeunt CHORUS *and* SILENUS *by Ramp B.*

NOTES ON THE TEXT

Minor uncertainties in the Greek text and slight alterations of the Greek for the sake of fluent English are not noted. The reader is referred to the introduction and the translator's foreword for discussion of the translation.

For a Greek text with facing literal translation, see David Kovacs, *Euripides* vol. 1, in the Loeb Classical Library (Cambridge, Mass., Harvard University Press, 1994). For the Greek text only, accompanied by a learned commentary and introduction, see Richard Seaford, *Euripides Cyclops* (Oxford: The Clarendon Press, 1984).

1–40 *prologue* The opening speech, recited in plain conversational meter, sets the scene for the action that follows. Silenus explains how he and his sons, the chorus of satyrs, find themselves slaves of Polyphemus in his savage home in Sicily.

6 *the jealous goddess Hera made you crazy* Hera was presumably jealous over Zeus' affair with Semele, Dionysus' mother; the story of Dionysus' madness is recounted by Apollodorus, *Library of Mythology* 3.5.1.

13–17 *enormous Enceladus . . . shared the war-spoils* Enceladus was one of the Giants (sons of Earth) who rose up against the Olympian gods and were defeated. The spoils stripped from Enceladus prove that Silenus didn't dream up the encounter.

19 *The torments can't be counted* On the number imagery, see translator's foreword.

20 *riled those pirates out of Tuscany* For the story, see the introduction.

41–83 (first choral song) The chorus of satyrs, who have entered by one of the two side ramps from the mountain pastures where they have been herding Polyphemus' sheep, sing a full-fledged choral ode (as opposed to the marching song, in anapestic meter, that is more typical of choral entrances). Accordingly, they would have performed relatively more intricate dance steps as they herded the animals into their pens.

45–46 *partied all the way to sweet Althaea's house* Althaea was Dionysus' daughter; nothing is known about the party.

74 *to strike up drinking songs* The Greek text at this point has the cry, Iacchos, Iacchos, a cult name of Bacchus used as an ecstatic exclamation.

84–402 (first episode) This section (technically, an episode is a passage in dialogue meter framed by two choral songs) begins with a scene involving Silenus and Odysseus, much of it in the line-for-line exchange called stichomythy. At line 197, Silenus exits, and the leader of the chorus continues the dialogue with Odysseus until Silenus' return at line 210. The arrival of Polyphemus at line 227 inaugurates a complex, four-way conversation among the Cyclops, Silenus, Odysseus, and the leader of the chorus, in which Silenus blames Odysseus for stealing Polyphemus' wares; the passage culminates in a pair of set speeches or *agôn*, in which Odysseus entreats the Cyclops to spare him and his men, and the Cyclops replies with a sophistic diatribe in defense of his bestial appetite. The episode ends with the Cyclops herding Odysseus and his sailors into the cave, visually recalling the end of the prologue in which the satyrs usher the sheep inside.

110 *son of Sisyphus* In some versions, Sisyphus, later condemned to push a rock up hill forever in the underworld, was Odysseus' father.

162–63 *Is there some magic way to make more wine flow in?* These two verses are missing in the manuscript; the supplement is anybody's guess (this one follows Kovacs).

188–89 *lovers' leap in old Leucadia* Leucadia was an island near Ithaca with steep limestone cliffs on its western side.

240 *I think I see Orion* The constellation of Orion, a famous hunter, was (and is) imagined as bearing a club.

303 *judge on Judgment Day* The Greek text has Rhadamanthus, one of the judges in the underworld.

388 *sea-salt* "Sea-salt" is Kovacs' supplement.

403–14 (second choral song) With the stage momentarily empty of actors, the chorus sings a brief ode in which they reveal their horror at Polyphemus' cannibalism.

417 *to the rotisserie . . .* A verse is missing from the chorus at this point in the Greek original.

417–532 (second episode) Odysseus emerges from the Cyclops' cave to recount the horrors he witnessed inside, largely in the kind of set piece conventionally called a messenger speech. He then discusses with the leader of the chorus his plan to blind Polyphemus.

487 *a lick or two* The Greek text is uncertain here.

533–79 (third choral song) This choral interlude begins with a brief anapestic song (the marching meter), followed by a lyric exchange between the chorus and Polyphemus, who exits drunk from his cave; in this part, the chorus sings a stanza, the Cyclops responds with another, and the chorus concludes with a third, all in a meter that is more like that of personal poetry than choral song. The style is that of the bawdy songs that were characteristic of the Greek symposium or drinking party (there is an amusing caricature of such a gathering at the end of Aristophanes' comedy, *The Wasps*).

537 *Singing from within* An ancient (and rare) stage direction, preserved in the Greek text.

572–676 (third episode) This scene begins with another series of stichomythic (line-for-line) exchanges involving Odysseus, Polyphemus and Silenus, in which the symposiastic spirit takes the slapstick form of horseplay round the wine jar, culminating in a pederastic assault by the Cyclops on Silenus. The episode ends with Odysseus' return into the cave.

582 *this Dionysus you've been drinking* Since Dionysus was associated with wine (among other things), one might refer to wine poetically by the god's name (usually in the form Bacchus).

653 *those Graces* Goddesses associated with beauty and charm.

652 *this charmer of a Ganymede* Ganymede was a Trojan youth beloved by Zeus and thus might symbolize a male (usually a boy) who was sexually

attractive to an adult man. Drunken ribaldry was characteristic of the classical Greek symposium in its more vulgar forms.

670 *Morpheus* The Greek has Hypnos, like Morpheus a personification of sleep.

674–87 (fourth choral song) A brief interlude while the stage is vacant.

688–726 (fourth episode) a brief scene between Odysseus and the chorus, which reveals its cowardice. The chorus is momentarily divided into two half-choruses, each presumably represented by a leader who speaks in the meter of dialogue.

718 *Orphic spell* An incantation like those connected with the cult of Orpheus, which involved secret mystical rites and belief in an afterlife.

723–40 (fifth choral song) This song fills the interval in which the stage is empty, between Odysseus' entry into the cave and the emergence of the blinded Cyclops.

777–827 (fifth and final episode) The blinded Cyclops is teased by the chorus leader, and after this horseplay Odysseus, his men, Silenus, and the chorus exit by the ramp leading toward the sea. The meter is that of dialogue throughout (the chorus has no separate exit march).

819–23 *Forget his miseries . . . multiply in luxury!* This passage is slightly amplified in respect to the original; see translator's foreword.

GLOSSARY

AETNA: a volcano in eastern Sicily, imagined in some traditions as the forge at which the Cyclopes manufactured Zeus' thunderbolts; in the *Cyclops*, the Cyclopes dwell on its slopes.

ALTHAEA: daughter of Dionysus and Dejanira (the wife of Hercules), according to one story.

APHRODITE: goddess of love and sexuality, born from the sea-foam (*aphros* in Greek) which was fertilized by the blood of her father, Uranus (Sky), after he was castrated by his son Zeus.

ATHENA: motherless daughter of Zeus, from whose head she is said to have sprung fully armed; she was the patron deity of Athens, and associated with crafts, warfare, and cultivation of the olive.

BACCHUS: another name for Dionysus.

CALYPSO: a sea-nymph; she dwelled on an isolated island, where she detained Odysseus for seven years during his voyage home to Ithaca.

CAPE MALEA: a promontory off the south of the Peloponnesus; its crosswinds and lack of harbors made it proverbially perilous for sailors.

CEPHALLENE: a large island to the west of Ithaca.

CYCLOPS: one of the one-eyed giants who lived, according to Homer (followed by Euripides), in caves, innocent of agriculture and seafaring as well as of political institutions. Another tradition identified them as sons of Uranus and Earth, and forgers of Zeus' thunderbolts.

DEMETER: a goddess associated with the cultivation of grain; she was a daughter of Cronus and Rhea, hence a sister of Zeus.

DIONYSUS: son of Zeus and the mortal Semele; associated with wine and festivity. Among his entourage were Silenus and the satyrs. He was also the patron deity of the theater in Athens.

ENCELADUS: one of the Giants; in the battle with the Olympian gods, Enceladus fought against Athena. He was buried under Mount Aetna and nourished its fires with his incinerated corpse.

GANYMEDE: a Trojan youth of whom Zeus became enamored; Zeus had him borne up to Mount Olympus on an eagle, where he made him the immortal cupbearer of the gods.

GIANTS: monstrous sons of Uranus and Earth, who rebelled against the hegemony of the Olympian deities.

GRACES: three minor goddesses associated with the ideal of beauty and charm.

HELEN: the wife of Menelaus, king of Sparta; she ran off with Paris, a son of Priam king of Troy, when he visited Sparta, and was thus the immediate cause of the Trojan War.

HEPHAESTUS: the lame son of Hera, whose particular province was the blacksmith's art; in one tradition, he had his forge on Mount Aetna.

HERA: Olympian goddess, wife (and sister) of Zeus; conventionally described as jealous over Zeus' philandering, as in the case of the mortal Semele, who bore Zeus' son Dionysus.

ILIUM: the city or citadel of Troy.

GLOSSARY

ITHACA: an island off the west coast of Greece, and the home of Odysseus.

LEUCADIA: an island near Ithaca, famous for its white limestone cliffs.

MARON: a priest of Apollo at Ismarus; when Odysseus raided the city on his way home from Troy, he spared Maron, who in gratitude gave him a casket of excellent wine.

MENELAUS: the king of Sparta and husband of Helen; his brother was Agamemnon, king of Mycenae and leader of the Greek forces at Troy.

MORPHEUS: a minor god personifying sleep; the Greek original has Hypnos (Sleep), which amounts to the same thing but is less familiar in English.

NAIADS: nymphs who inhabited springs or brooks.

NEREIDS: sea nymphs and daughters of Nereus.

NEREUS: a marine deity, son of Earth and Sea; sometimes called The Old Man of the Sea.

ODYSSEUS: the protagonist of Homer's *Odyssey*, where he is the son of Laertes (rather than of Sisyphus) and ruler of Ithaca. He was renowned for his wiliness as well as for his strength and courage (the strategem of the Trojan Horse was attributed to him). In Homer's *Iliad*, he is the leader of the Ithacan troops at Troy; the *Odyssey* describes his adventures on his voyage home.

OLYMPUS: a mountain in northern Greece, imagined as the home of Zeus and the gods of his generation (hence the designation Olympian).

ORION: a giant hunter, transformed after his death into a constellation.

ORPHIC: pertaining to Orpheus, a mythical singer associated also with mystical rites, magic, and survival in the afterlife; hence Orphic spell.

PHRYGIA: the region in which Troy was located.

POLYPHEMUS: a Cyclops, and son of Poseidon; although the Cyclopes are solitary cave dwellers, Polyphemus appears to be the chief among them in Homer's *Odyssey*.

POSEIDON: an Olympian god whose chief domain was the sea; he was also associated with earthquakes. In Homer's *Odyssey*, he is represented as the father of Polyphemus and the cause of Odysseus' subsequent wanderings.

PRIAM: king of Troy at the time of the Trojan War; slain after the capture of the city by the Greeks.

SATYR: woodland deities, human in form but often imagined as having the ears, horns, tail, and legs of goats. They were associated with Dionysus' retinue, and sometimes (as in the *Cyclops*) represented as sons of Silenus. They formed the regular chorus in satyr plays, hence the name.

SICILY: a large, triangular island south of the boot of Italy. In classical times, it was inhabited by native populations in the interior; several Greek cities were located on its shores, including one near the slopes of Mount Aetna. The Cyclopes were imagined as residing there in mythical times.

SILENUS: a fat, satyrlike, boozy companion of Dionysus, sometimes represented as Dionysus' foster-son and father, in turn, of the satyrs.

SISYPHUS: a king of Corinth, noted for his cunning; in some traditions he is represented as Odysseus' father. He was punished in the underworld by having to roll a heavy stone endlessly uphill.

SUNIUM: a promontory in the south of Attica (the territory round the city of Athens).

TAENARUM: a promontory on the south of the Peloponnesus, west of Cape Malea.

TRITON: a sea god, son of Poseidon and Amphitrite, sometimes imagined as having the tail of a sea serpent and tooting on a large conch.

TROJAN: an inhabitant of Troy.

TROY: a city (or its territory) near the Helespont, where the Greeks fought a ten-year campaign to avenge the abduction of Helen. Odysseus is on his way home from this war when he puts in at the Cyclops' territory.

ZEUS: the ruler of the Olympian gods, husband of Hera. His special domain was the sky, where he wielded the thunderbolt; he was believed to favor the just and was the patron deity of guests and strangers.

Printed in the United States
203828BV00001B/31-72/A

9 780195 143034